I0202988

Love Songs in Spanish for Enjoyment and Learning

Robert Stuart Thomson

Copyright © 2015-2020 by Robert Stuart Thomson

All rights reserved. No part of this publication may be reproduced, stored in a retrieval system, or transmitted, in any form or by any means, electronic, mechanical, photocopying, recording, or otherwise, without the written prior permission of the publisher.

Published by Godwin Books, Victoria, B.C.
www.godwinbooks.com

Library and Archives Canada Cataloguing in Publication

Thomson, Robert Stuart, 1940-, author

Love Songs in Spanish for Enjoyment and Learning / Robert Stuart Thomson.

Includes bibliographical references.

ISBN 978-0-9696774-9-9 (paperback)

1. Spanish language--Textbooks for second language learners--

English speakers. 2. Spanish language--Sound recordings for

English speakers. 3. Love songs. 4. Songs, Spanish. I. Title.

PC4129.E5T56 2015   468.3'421   C2015-905505-9

Editing by Dr. Derek Carr

Cover design by Iryna Spica
Typeset in *Queens Park* at SpicaBookDesign

Printed with KDP

What Some Readers Have Said

This book contains a selection of twenty-four beautiful Spanish language boleros, tangos, rancheras and other love songs. There are such classics as Gardel's "Mi Buenos Aires Querido", Agustin Lara's "Granada", Ernesto Lecuona's "Siboney" and the birthday standard "Las Mañanitas." (...) Each of the twenty-four lessons is accompanied by black-and-white photographs of the composer or performer; a Spanish song lyric with an English translation; Thomson's notes about the historical context of each composition; his interpretation of the song's meaning, and grammar and lexicon-related outlines (e.g. about idioms). I wholeheartedly agree [with Thomson] that target language songs can provide a memorable, emotion-charged teaching method. Thomson's Love Songs in Spanish for Enjoyment and Learning is an inspired project that could successfully be used to add an enjoyable cultural component in many beginning, intermediate or even advanced Spanish language classes in the hands of a skilled teacher. ~ Elena Retzer, California State University in Los Angeles, writing in "Hispania," a journal for the Spanish language. December, 2016

You have compiled a wonderful array of songs and it's great to have the words and stories with them. ~ Gabriela McBee (University of Victoria, B.C.)

This book is much more than a collection of twenty-four love songs. Spanish instructors wanting to infuse their classes with a unique approach to learning Spanish, students wanting to gain an edge by learning informal language and travelers who wish to connect in Spanish with people in Latin American or Spain will enjoy Thomson's latest book. The book encompasses several genres and represents a variety of Spanish-speaking countries. (...) For the translation of the song lyrics from Spanish into English, Thomson uses the classic interlinear format so that the Spanish words align with the English, thereby helping readers to make connections. Multiple comments on the lives of composers, lyricists and recording artists enrich the text. [So do] Thomson's comments on the significance of such things as the changes from minor to major key and the atmosphere created by the solo trumpet in "Granada". The main emphasis is always on fostering comprehension of the language in depth. Additional support materials are the sections What to appreciate in a song,

Endearments in Spanish, Historical origins of the language of love, How Nat King Cole came to sing in Spanish, Using cloze outlines to teach songs, Suggested projects and reports for class presentation. ~ Eileen M. Angelini, Canisius College, Buffalo, New York writing in The Review of the Northeast Conference of Teachers of Foreign Languages, September, 2016 (number 78).

Tu libro me gusta mucho y la selección de canciones que incluye. De tu presentación me gustó en particular la forma en que explicabas la historia de las canciones, el momento que estaban viviendo los compositores al escribirlas. ~ Patricia Castañeda

You have a beautiful and unique book here and it all comes from your mind, soul, and hard work!
~ Agustín Luviano-Cordero (Victoria B.C.)

I am thrilled with your book! ~ Lucy Orihuel (Sarasota, Florida)

Lo felicito a usted por su gran método de enseñanza. ¡Es fantástico! Las canciones son maravillosas. ¡Imagino lo mucho que sus alumnos las aprecian mucho y disfrutan la clase! ~ Zuri Aguirre (Tepic, Mexico)

Robert, ¡Excelente trabajo! ¡Muchas felicidades! ~ Ana Lucia Joch, Guadalajara and Puerto Vallarta.

As a teacher of Spanish I found this book very helpful in teaching and re-enforcing grammar points to students. ~ Nora Robson, teacher of Spanish (Victoria B.C.)

Robert Stuart Thomson

Author's Preface

to "Love Songs in Spanish for Enjoyment and Learning" (An Audio-visual Approach)

"A thing of beauty is a joy forever."
John Keats, 1795-1821

The twenty-four songs in this book have been selected for the beauty of their music and the poetic quality of their lyrics. They come mostly from Latin-America although two are from Spain. They cover many aspects of that sometimes very strange thing which mortals call "love".

This book had its origins in the late 1970s although I certainly did not know it at the time. It was then that I started going to Mexico for a vacation every winter. There were the usual attractions: the sunny weather, the beaches and the exotic people. But there was more that that: I soon became enamoured with Spanish and the lovely songs that seemed to be played wherever I went. Before long I bought cassettes of Eydie Gorme and Vicente Fernández and once back in Vancouver listened to them over and over again on my twenty-five mile commute. A Mexican friend helped me with the translation of the songs and I was well on my way to improving my accent and oral comprehension, learning new vocabulary and finding out about the Mexican attitude towards life and love as reflected in their songs. Before I knew it the auditory cortex had performed its magic and I had some of them memorized. It was proving to be a most enjoyable experience; it was also an enjoyable way to learn Spanish.

There came a time when I wanted to read some good books on these songs and their background. Who wrote them? What were Eydie Gorme and Vicente Fernández all about? To my surprise there was nothing available. There were a few biographies of composers and recording artists but no one book containing the information I wanted: the Spanish lyrics, a good translation, notes on language difficulties, and observations on the poetic elements: similes, metaphors, personification, pathetic fallacies, etc. I would also include notes (with photos) on the composer, the librettist, and the recording artist, and would suggest to readers which artists to listen to by googling the title of the song on Youtube. This set me thinking: Why not write the kind of book that I was looking for? So I set about it.

I decided to focus on love in its many guises and I chose twenty-four songs. They included a variety: boleros (or rumbas), tangos, cha-chas, ranchera songs, and Viennese waltzes. The songs were from several Spanish-speaking countries: Mexico first and foremost because I knew its music best, but there were also songs from Panamá, Argentina, Venezuela, Puerto Rico, the Dominican Republic, Cuba and Spain. I did not set out to limit my choice of songs to the Golden Era, *la Época de Oro*, (approximately 1930 to 1955) but as things turned out most of them are from that time frame which produced such a rich vein of lyricism.

And so it came to pass. Each of the twenty-four songs in *Love Songs in Spanish for Enjoyment and Learning* explores a distinctive aspect of love. *Solamente una vez* (song 1) contends that you have only one great love in life; *¡Amor! ¡amor!* (song 2) claims that love comes from God and the soul; *Noche de ronda* (song 3) reveals a man on a balcony looking up at the moon doing its rounds and wondering if the lady who just left him is doing the same thing; *¿Quizás? ¿quizás?* (song 4) is about a lover who is stuck on a girl who is maddeningly commitment-shy; *Cielito lindo* (song 5) is a warning to men: if you leave the nest and try to return years later don't be surprised if it is occupied by another man; *Sabor a mí* (song 10) makes the point that lovers who connect at the deepest of levels will be marked by that love forever, even after they part. A tango, *Caminito* (song 11), is the story of a man who returns to the rural pathway on which his lady and

he used to take walks. Alas! she has gone forever and he has only the pathway to confide in. *Se me olvidó otra vez* (song 16) is about losing someone and refusing to leave the old haunts in the vain hope that she will return some day. *Granada* (song 17) is Agustín Lara's salute to his Spanish heritage and the famous Andalusian city. The other fifteen songs also explore the labyrinth of love and whether inspired by elation or despair they make for compelling listening.

The recording artists I recommend are the best I know of: Eydie Gorme (with the brilliant Trio Los Panchos), Lola Beltrán ('Lola la Grande'), Vicente Fernández, Plácido Domingo, Julio Iglesias and Carlos Gardel. And there are others. Look for them in Youtube (they will appear on the right side of your screen). I think most readers will appreciate Nat King Cole singing *¿Quizás? ¿quizás?* when they know that he got the idea of singing in Spanish through a chance encounter when he was on tour in Germany. Be sure to listen to (and watch) Luis Miguel doing a passionate rendition of *Y qué hiciste del amor que me juraste?*

I wrote this book primarily to show readers what a joy it is to listen to a beautiful Spanish song and understand every word and all the nuances. I also hope that students of Spanish will find it a useful tool for learning. For this reason I have included a section called "General Notes" and another called "Language points". "General Notes" includes such things as the composer, the historical background, and the meaning of the song. "Language

Points" supplies information on grammar, usage, verb tenses, and idioms. My explanations are not exhaustive and **I have assumed that the language student will have a good grammar book close at hand.**

If you are a teacher thinking of using songs in your language program, I highly recommend that you do so. Your students will love them. (And wouldn't it be great if studying these songs led your students to an appreciation of the many great ballads written in America in that same fertile 1930-1955 time frame: memorable songs such as *Begin the Beguine, These Foolish Things, As Time Goes By, The Summer Wind, The Shadow of your Smile,* and *Cry Me a River?*) I have included a section called "What to appreciate in the songs" (pp. 11-12) and at the end of the book you will find a detailed section on how to set up the classroom and the steps to follow when presenting the material (whether using cloze outlines or the complete text).

Several of the songs can be used to teach verb tenses, idioms, etc. *Cucurrucucú, paloma* (song 8) makes a good exercise on the imperfect tense. *Piel canela* (song 13) provides an excellent overview of the

subjunctive. *Miraron llorar* (song 12) presents some interesting idioms. *Caminito* (song 10) is a poignant romantic poem and would fit well in a discussion of Romantic poetry.

Having searched the internet many times for the Spanish words to these songs I have concluded that many versions are unreliable and that the interested reader would welcome an accurate version. This is yet another reason why I wrote this book.

One walks a tightrope in trying to write one book for all levels of readers but I do believe that the beginner will find this book accessible and that all readers, even the advanced ones, will find it interesting.

I recommend frequent reviews of those songs which you have already studied. Keep at it and you will have them memorized before you know it. Many of them are fine poems and like all fine poems they will become a treasured part of your storehouse of memories.

For a list of the people shown on the cover of this book see page 126.

Robert Stuart Thomson, Ph.D.

See my site: **www.godwinbooks.com** for my writings, especially those which involve studying songs and opera: *Great Songs for the English Classroom* (1980), *Italian for the Opera* (1991), and *Operatic Italian* (2009). My e-mail is rthomson@islandnet.com and I welcome letters.

Acknowledgements

Several people have helped me with this book. I wish to express my gratitude to Allen Specht for his overall excellent advice on several points; to Augustin Luviano-Cordero for editing; to Alfonso (Poncho) Martínez (a.k.a. Mr. Jackson) in Puerto Vallarta, for his help with recording the songs; to Ana Cheimak at the Victoria Public Library for her insider's information on Buenos Aires; to Carlos Salza, owner of Buenos Aires Walking Tours, for clarifying some points of language. Thank you to Zuri Aguirre and Adriana Bedolla at the Amistad Club in Puerto Vallarta for trying out my method in their classroom. Finally, my thanks to Ana Lucia Joch for her help with some fine points of language. The formating of this book is the typically outstanding work of Iryna Spica of SpicaBookDesign in Victoria, B.C.

Table of Contents

1.
Solamente una vez

Agustín Lara, Mexico, 1935

Artist: Manuelita Arriola

Agustín Lara

1. Solamente una vez
Only once

2. amé en la vida.
I have loved in life.

3. Solamente una vez
Only once

4. y nada más.
and nothing more (i.e. no more than that)

5. Una vez, nada más
Once, no more than that

6. en mi huerto
in my garden (or orchard)

7. brilló la esperanza,
shone hope (did hope shine)

8. la esperanza que alumbra
hope which lights up

9. el camino de mi soledad.
the pathway of my loneliness.

10. Una vez, nada más, se entrega el alma
Once, no more than that, does one give one's own soul

11. con la dulce y total renunciación.
with sweet and total renunciation.

12. Y cuando ese milagro realiza
And when that miracle produces

13. el prodigio de amarse
the prodigious phenomenon of two people loving each other

14. hay campanas de fiesta
There are festival church bells

15. que cantan en el corazón.
that sing in the heart.

Repeat 10-15

Robert Stuart Thomson

General Notes

For each song I am including a section called "General Notes" for background information on the songs and a second section (see below) called "Language Points" to explain some of the main points about grammar and idioms. This section does not pretend to be complete; it is only a general guide.

Language Points

- line **2**: *amé,* and *brilló* (line **7**) are in the preterite/pretérito (simple past) verb tense. Because of the demands of the music *amé* and *en* (line **2**) have to be combined in order to fit into two syllables i. e. the "e" of "en" is dropped, leaving *amén.*

- line **10**: *se entrega* from *entregarse,* to deliver oneself, to give oneself. A reflexive verb.

- line **13**: *el prodigio de amarse:* the prodigious phenomenon of two people loving each other. Spanish is often flowery and elegant but at times it can be terse and say a great deal with few words, as it does here. The meaning might be illuminated by this line of Juliet's when she ponders on the implications of loving Romeo:

> "Prodigious birth of love it is to me
> That I must love a loathed enemy."
>
> Juliet in *Romeo and Juliet*

Ana María González

Agustín Lara and the Birth of *Solamente una vez*

Agustín Lara was born in 1897, possibly in Mexico City, possibly Veracruz. His mother died when he was very young and his father disappeared early from the scene leaving Lara to be brought up by an aunt. Lara was precocious and began singing and playing piano in bars and bordellos in his mid-teens. In 1933 he toured Cuba, discovered the rumba, and played an important part in importing that stately dance to Mexico. Lara wrote hundreds of songs, the most memorable of which are, in my opinion, *Solamente una vez, Noche de ronda, Granada, María Bonita,* and *Nací con alma de pirata.* Apart from *Solamente una vez* I have included

Lara's white art deco house in Veracruz has been turned into a museum to honor him. It is well worth a visit, preferably on a moonlit night.

two other Lara songs in this book: *Noche de ronda* (song 3) and *Granada* (song 17). The Spanish admired Lara and Franco gave Lara a house in Granada in recognition for writing the famous song of the same name. Lara's white art deco house in Veracruz has been turned into a museum to honor him. It is well worth a visit, preferably on a moonlit night.

The birth of *Solamente una vez* is interesting. Lara was on a musical tour of South America in 1935 and he was in love with the group's singer, Ana María González.

(see photo on p. 3). They had terrible fights and after one of these fights Ana María threatened to leave and go back to Mexico. Lara thought this would be disastrous for the group (and very sad for himself) so he wrote her a song which would convince her of his love and cause her to stay with the tour. Whatever his motives, the song did the trick and she stayed on. *Solamente una vez* is featured in two movies: *Los tres caballeros* and *Melodía de américa* There is also a movie which celebrates Lara's most famous compositions: *La vida de Lara* (1958).

In a movie on the life of Frida Kahlo (*Frida, naturaleza viva*, 1983, with Ofelia Medina in the title role) there is a scene near the end in which Frida and a German girl-friend start singing *Solamente una vez* while preparing supper. This song is iconic in Mexico. The mention of *campanas* (line 14) is a rich allusion; church bells are a delight to hear in Mexico.

Manuelita Arriola

My recommended vocalist is Manuelita Arriola (1920-2004) who was born in Rosario (Sinaloa), Mexico. She was at her prime in the 1940s. You can listen to her and maybe even see her in action by googling "YouTube and Manuelita Arriola."

How to Approach Each Song

1. Google Youtube and find a good version of the song you are going to work on. Some versions will show you the artist singing the song, others won't. For the words see song number one in this book.

2. As you listen to the song follow the words to it in this book. I find it helps to point to the words with a pencil as I hear them. Say the words out loud. Repeat this process several times. Talk (or even better, sing) along with the singer. Imitate as closely as you can his/her pronunciation and phrasing (the rhythmic rise and fall of the sentences). Spanish has lovely musical cadences which you should try to make your own.

3. As you read the Spanish words use the English translation to help you. Try to see the connections between the two versions: the meanings of the words and such things as verb tenses, idioms and grammar points.

4. As you go deeper into each song you will find it satisfying to appreciate such things as aspects of culture, message, poetic devices, innuendo, suggestive power, orchestration and instruments used, quality of the singer's (or singers') voice/s, etc. (For details on these issues see the section "What to look for in the songs.")

Veracruz in Mexico

5. I wouldn't spend too much time on each song (listen to it maybe four or five times), but would go on to the next song and repeat the process outlined above. When you have finished working on the second song, repeat the first song and then go on to song number three. This way you are continually reviewing as you learn new songs. Constant review is important because it enables you to make these songs your very own. What a worthwhile accomplishment! When you are in a restaurant or on a beach in Mexico and the mariachis come by, you can now order one of your favorite new songs and sing along with them. Your knowledge of the original lyrics will endear you to them and to any native speakers who observe what is going on. You are acknowledging something beautiful and distinctive in their culture.

2.
¡Amor! ¡amor! ¡amor!

Gabriel Ruiz, Mexico, 1944

Artists: Eydie Gorme and the Trío los Panchos

1. ¡Amor! ¡amor! ¡amor!
Love! Love! Love!

2. nació de ti, nació de mí,
It was born of you, it was born of me,

3. de la esperanza!
(it was born) of hope!

4. ¡Amor! ¡amor! ¡amor!
Love! Love! Love!

5. nació de Diós, para los dos,
It was born of God, for the two of us,

6. nació del alma.
It was born of the soul

CHORUS

7. Sentir que tus besos se anidaron en mí
To feel that your kisses made their nest in me

8. igual que palomas mensajeras de luz.
Just like doves, messengers of light,

9. Saber que mis besos se quedaron en ti
To know that my kisses stayed with you

10. haciendo en tus labios la señal de la cruz.
Making on your lips the sign of the cross.

Repeat verses 10 then 1-6.

General Notes

Although secular in theme *¡Amor! ¡amor!* contains many religious words and allusions: *Dios, esperanza, alma, nacer, paloma, la señal de la cruz*. Catholicism left a profound mark on the Latin-American mindcast and you find many Christian allusions even in secular songs like *¡Amor! ¡amor!* In our first song, *Solamente una vez*, the church bells (lines **14-15**) remind us of Catholicism. In several of our songs one finds the idealism of Christianity transposed to love between man and woman.

Gabriel Ruiz

The composer of *¡Amor! ¡amor!* is Gabriel Ruiz, the lyrics are the creation of López Méndez. Ruiz was born in Guadalajara in 1914. At age twenty he gave up studying law to become a concert pianist, a music teacher and a song writer. He started his singing career in Mazatlán. *¡Amor! ¡amor!* dates from 1944 and was featured in an American film, *Broadway Rhythm* (1944), starring George Murphy.

Language Points

- lines **2** and **7**. *nació* (line **2**) and *anidaron* (from *anidarse*, to make one's nest, line **7**) are both in the preterite (simple past).

Many of the best love songs in Spanish were recast into English to make them acceptable (or so the song-adapters thought) in English-speaking countries. The following is typical of many. You can see how far it strays in meaning from the original Spanish version. It is a shame but English-speaking people who listen to these altered versions probably assume that they closely resemble the original Spanish versions.

Here are the words of the American version of *Amor, Amor, Amor!* It is nothing like the original and there is nothing spiritual about it. Ay, ¡qué bárbaro! However, the beautiful melody is the same in both languages and this is probably why some astute marketer decided that the song could be successful in the United States, Canada, etc.

1. Amor, amor, amor…

2. This word so sweet

3. That I repeat,

4. Means I adore you.

5. Amor, amor, my love…

6. Would you deny

7. That heart that I

8. Have placed before you?

9. I can't find another word

10. With meaning so clear;

11. My lips try to whisper

12. Sweeter things in your ear,

13. But somehow or other

14. Nothing sounds quite so dear

15. As this soft caressing word I know.

16. Amor, amor, my love…

17. When you're away

18. There is no day

19. And nights are lonely.

20. Amor, amor, my love…

21. Say you'll be mine

22. And love me only.

Eydie Gorme

One of the best recording artists of this song (and many other love songs in Spanish) is the American, Eydie Gorme.

Eydie was born in the Bronx in 1931 of immigrant parents of Sephardic Jewish origin and grew up speaking Spanish fluently, which was to serve her well in her career. In 1957 she married the crooner, Steve Lawrence, and went on many tours with him. Her 1963 hit, *Blame it on the Bossa Nova,* sold over a million records. Fortune smiled on her again in 1964 when she wisely teamed up with the talented *Trío Los Panchos* and produced the hit album *Sabor a mí* (song 10 below), a priceless album of love songs in Spanish. Eydie died in 2013.

What to Appreciate in the Songs

As you work on the songs here are some suggested criteria:

Words (lyrics):

Does the song have a message? What is it about (idealistic love, unrequited love, malicious gossip, etc.)?

Are the ideas complex enough to develop a theme? Does it rely too much on repetition? (Songs 19 and 20 are good examples of complex development.)

What does the song reflect about the culture which gave rise to it? What makes the song typically Mexican, Argentinian, Catholic, tropical, etc.? For example, song 9 contains much Christian imagery; song 16 is typical of the 1940s in some ways.

Are there poetic devices (similes, metaphors, etc.)? Are they used effectively? (e.g. good metaphors are found in songs 8 and 19.)

Does the songwriter use personification and apostrophe i.e. the 'pathetic fallacy' (e.g. songs 2, 11, 20.)?

Do some words have innuendos, suggestive power or literary echoes (See song 15)? Are affectionate diminutives used well (e. g. song 20)?

Are there any rare or unusual words? Do they add anything to the song?

Are some of the words impossible to translate directly?

Are the lyrics original or unusual?

Is repetition used to good effect (e.g. songs 2 and 11)?

Is impressionism used as a technique (e.g. songs 17, 20, 21, 22)?

Music:

Does the music seem original?

Is it pleasing?

Does it create a mood or an atmosphere?

Is there an introduction and if there is does it add anything to the song e.g. does it create an appropriate atmosphere? Does it provide effective contrast with the rest of the song? Is it in a minor key and thereby contrasts nicely with the rest of the song which might be in a major key?

Are minor and major keys used effectively e.g. is a minor key used to create an atmosphere of sadness, loneliness, etc. (See song 3)?

Are key changes used effectively elsewhere in the song e. g. for variety or to intensify emotion (e.g. song 7, lines. **4-5**)?

Is variety conveyed by switching from solo to duet, or from solo to chorus?

Is variety conveyed by alternating male and female voices or by alternating voice and musical instruments?

Are musical instruments used effectively? Do they create a mood or reinforce a theme (e.g. songs 17, 19)?

What is the singer like? Evaluate his/her interpretation. How does it compare with interpretations by other artists? (You will find them on *YouTube.*)

Is any group (e.g., Trío los Panchos) involved in the singing? Evaluate them.

Mariachis playing at the Tenampa in Mexico City

3.
Noche de ronda

Agustín Lara, Mexico, 1935

Artists: Eydie Gorme and the Trío los Panchos

NOCHE DE RONDA
(Be Mine Tonight)

Original Words and Music by MARÍA TERESA LARA
English Words by SUNNY SKYLAR

Moderately

No - che   de   ron - da, _____ The   night   is
¡No - che   de   ron - da, _____ qué   tris - te

wak - ing, _____ My   arms   are
pa - sas, _____ qué   tris - te

INTRODUCTION

1. **Noche de ronda, ¡qué triste pasas!**
Night of the rounds, how sad(ly) you pass by!

2. **¡Qué triste cruzas por mi balcón!**
How sad(ly) you cross my balcony!

3. **Noche de ronda, ¡cómo me hieres!**
Night of the rounds, how you wound me!

4. **¡Cómo lastimas mi corazón!**
How you hurt my heart!

REFRAIN

5. **Luna que se quiebra sobre la tiniebla de mi soledad**
Oh moon who breaks in pieces over the shadow of my solitude,

6. **¿Adónde vas?**
Where are you going?

7. **Dime si esta noche tu te vas de ronda como ella se fue,**
Tell me if this night you are doing the rounds just like she left,

8. **¿Con quién está?**
With whom she is.

9. **Dile que la quiero, dile que me muero de tanto esperar.**
Tell her that I love her, tell her that I am dying from waiting so long.

10. **¡Qué vuelva ya!**
May she return!

11. **que las rondas no son buenas,**
for the rounds are not good

12. **que hacen daño, que dan penas**
For they cause damage and give pain

13. **y se acaba por llorar.**
and one ends up weeping.

Repeat vv. 5-13

General Notes

Imagine Agustín Lara standing alone on the balcony of his white art deco home in south Veracruz. It is evening and he looks out over the waters of the Gulf of Mexico. He looks up at the moon, fatefully following her nightly path, changing nightly but implacably on course. Then he starts to think of his loneliness, his solitude and the fact that, *a pesar de todo* (in spite of everything) he sorely misses the lady who was in his life.

"Whither goest thou, oh moon?" (*¿A dónde vas?*). Are you doing the rounds of the taverns up there with the same fateful determination with which she left me? (*como ella se fue*). I'll bet that she is doing the rounds as well, of the night clubs! And just who is she with now?" (*Con quién está?*) You could say that Lara too is doing the rounds, mentally, out on that balcony. And it isn't just what Lara says outright (e.g. *se fue*) but what is suggested, that she is unreliable and a bit of a rover. He is reduced to the desperate measure of asking the moon to intercede on his behalf and bring the lady back. Go and shoot thy shafts, Diana the Huntress! See if you can hit her with one!

Noche de ronda is one of the most poetic, suggestive and elusive songs that I have ever encountered. Lara creates the magic, both the music and the words, and how well they fit together! As you listen to this song it is amusing to let your imagination wander and see where it takes you. The connotations of *las rondas* are rich: a sentry does his rounds, a child sings and dances a *ronda* (Is it suggested that love is often but a childish game?), people in a bar offer a round of drinks. And so on. *Luna* is rich in associations: lunacy, lunatic, etc. To carry a torch for this woman, is it not folly?

How is it that a difficult, womanizing, lounge-lizard like Lara can write songs like an angel? Who knows? Salieri wondered the same thing about Mozart in the movie *Amadeus*. People have wondered for years about that arch-moocher, Richard Wagner.

Lara uses the minor and major keys skillfully. The first four verses are sung lento and in the minor key, conveying sadness, separation, doubts and fear. With verse five we are suddenly in the major key which is more affirmative and a fit vehicle for carrying the narrator's forceful questioning of the moon.

Language Points

Throughout this song there are many verbs in the present tense: *pasas* (line **1**); *cruzas* (line **2**); *hieres* (line **3**); *lastimas* (line **4**); *se quiebra* (from *quebrarse*, line **5**); also: *vas, vas, está, son, hacen, dan*. This song would make a good exercise on verbs in the present tense.

- line **2**: *por mi balcón. Por* here means "over". Spanish prepositions are sometimes totally different from their English equivalents.

- line **5**: *quebrarse* suggests something shattering (literally and figuratively). It can be used to describe a voice which is trembling with emotion: *Se le quebró la voz con la emoción.* (His voice trembled with emotion.) The moonlight shows itself at intervals, unpredictably, probably much like the lady he is agonizing over.

- line **7**: *como ella se fue.* The sense is something like 'Tell me if this night you are fatefully doing the rounds just like she fatefully left.' i.e. both the moon and the lady can't help repeating what they do.

- line **8**: i. e. Hey, tell me this too: Who is she with right now?

- line **9**: Spanish can be florid but it also can be terse, as in this line.

- line **10**: *vuelva* (from *volver*) is a subjunctive of wish i.e. "May she come back!"

- line **13** *se acaba* from *acabarse:* to end up, to finish by, etc. Spanish uses lots of reflexive verbs. See also line 9: *me muero,* from *morirse,* to die.

The Americanized version starts as follows:

1. Noche de ronda, the night is waking,

2. My arms are aching. (…)

5. See the setting sun, the evening's just begun and love is in the air.

6. Be mine tonight, etc.

_____

_____

_____

_____

_____

_____

_____

4.
¿Quizás? ¿quizás? ¿quizás?

Osvaldo Farrés, Cuba, 1947

Artist: Nat King Cole

Osvaldo Farrés

1. Siempre que te pregunto que cuándo, cómo, y dónde,
   Whenever I ask when, how, and where

2. Tú siempre me respondes, "¿Quizás? ¿quizás? ¿quizás?"
   you always answer me: "Perhaps. Perhaps. Perhaps."

3. Y así pasan los días y yo, desesperando,
   And thus the days go by and I, despairing,

4. Y tú, tú contestando, "¿Quizás? ¿quizás? ¿quizás?"
   and you, answering, "Perhaps. Perhaps. Perhaps."

5. Estás perdiendo el tiempo, pensando, pensando.
   You are wasting time, thinking, thinking.

6. Por lo que más tú quieras, ¿hasta cuándo? ¿hasta cuándo?
   For heaven's sake, how long, how long?

7. Y así pasan los días, y yo, desesperando,
   And thus the days go by and I, despairing,

8. Y tú, y tú contestando, "¿Quizás? ¿quizás? ¿quizás?"
   and you answering, "Perhaps. Perhaps. Perhaps."

   Repeat 7-8, then 5-8.

General Notes

Osvaldo Farrés was born in 1903 in Quemado de Güines, a small city in the heart of Cuba. He became a composer of note even though he never learned to read music or play the piano. In 1962 Farrés and his wife left Cuba for good and spent the rest of their lives in New Jersey. He composed many songs. Among the best known are *Tres palabras, Acércate más (Come closer)*, *¿Quizás? ¿quizás?* and *Madrecita* (1954). *Acércate mas* (1940) became the theme song of an American movie, *Come Closer*, starring Esther Williams. *Madrecita* has become popular throughout Latin America as part of the celebration of Mother's Day. Farrés died in 1985.

During a trip to Germany in the early 1950s Nat went to a nightclub and heard a German sing uncannily well in English a few of Nat's songs. When the German joined the Coles at their table he needed an interpreter to communicate with them in English. Cole was astounded. This experience led eventually to Cole's studying Latin-American songs carefully enough so that he could deliver them clearly and with great poise on his recordings and on his 1958 trip to Cuba and South America. (The Cubans were so taken with Nat's delivery that many of them went around town speaking with Cole's accent.)

Nat King Cole, Joan Crawford, Al Steele, Francois Baguer and Mrs. Emilio Bacardi at Havana's Tropicana Night Club. 1956

Months later, in Brazil, about sixty thousand people turned out for Nat's concert in a soccer stadium. Many of those who attended could hardly afford it. Nat realized this and was profoundly moved by their generous reception. He later said that this was the most gratifying event in his life.

It is a pity that Americans for the most part were unaware of Cole's triumphant tour south and knew very little about the many excellent songs in Spanish which he had recorded. They might have known the versions in English but these were a pale reflection of the originals.

Language Points

- line **6**: "Por lo que más tu quieras" is an idiom and should be translated by one, e.g. "For heaven's sake".

Version in English for the North American market:

1. You won't admit you love me and so how am I ever.

2. To know. You always tell me, "Perhaps, perhaps, perhaps."

3. A million times I've asked you and then I ask you over.

4. Again you only answer, "Perhaps, perhaps, perhaps." etc.

5.
Cielito lindo

Quirino Mendoza y Cortés, Mexico, 1882

Artists: El Mariachi Vargas

El Mariachi Vargas. 1940s

1. **De la Sierra Morena, Cielito lindo,**
From the Sierra Morena, 'Pretty Little Heaven,'

2. **vienen bajando**
are descending

3. **un par de ojitos negros**
a pair of nice dark eyes,

4. **Cielito lindo, de contrabando.**
Pretty Little Heaven, (and they are) contraband.

Repeat 1-4

CHORUS (5-7)

5. **¡Ay, ay, ay, ay! ¡Canta y no llores!**
Ay, ay, ay, ay! Sing and don't cry!

6. **Porque cantando se alegran,**
Because by singing become happy,

7. **Cielito lindo, los corazones.**
Pretty Little Heaven, hearts.

5-7 In normal prose: Sing and don't cry, Pretty Little Heaven, because hearts become happy by singing.

Repeat 5-7

8. **Ese lunar que tienes,**
That beauty spot that you have,

9. **Cielito lindo, junto a la boca,**
Pretty Little Heaven, next to your mouth

10. **no se lo des a nadie**
Don't give it to anybody

11. **Cielito lindo, que a mí me toca.**
Pretty Little Heaven, it belongs to me.

Repeat 8-11; then 5-7 (twice)

We have included an extra verse (12-15) here but it is not on your CD.

12. **Pájaro que abandona,**
A bird which abandons,

13. **Cielito lindo, su primer nido,**
Pretty Little Heaven, its first nest,

14. **si lo encuentra ocupado,**
If it finds it occupied,

15. **Cielito lindo, bien merecido.**
Pretty Little Heaven, (it's) well deserved

Robert Stuart Thomson

Quirino
Mendoza
y Cortés
(1859-1957),
composer of
"Cielito lindo"

General Notes

There are many verses to this song and I have included only a few of them.

Cielito lindo is in keeping with the commonly held idea (at least in Mexico) that certain regions of the country produce the most beautiful women. I recall chatting with a taxi driver in Guadalajara who went into raptures telling me that the most beautiful women in Mexico came from a hill town on the edge of Guadalajara.

Cielito lindo is typical of those phrases that elude accurate translation but if you learn them in their Spanish context you get a feel for what they mean.

There is a golden moment in the Three Tenors Concert (Baths of Caracalla, 1990) when Plácido Domingo bursts into *Cielito lindo* and Pavarotti, apparently surprised at the choice, grins at him with absolute delight. (This is found in the Finale medley of the concert.) *Cielito lindo* is featured in the movie, *Los tres Garcia*, starring Pedro Infante.

I recommend you search Youtube for the Mariachi Vargas rendition of this song. The Vargas group dates back to 1897 and has a long history as one of the best mariachi groups in Mexico. In 1934 they accompanied the progressive president of Mexico, Lázaro Cárdenas, on his campaign tour.

I just did a google search using the search phrase "endearments in Spanish" and it came up with about forty of them, with translations (or, most often, paraphrases, because they often defy translation). I have listed some of the more common ones on the next page.

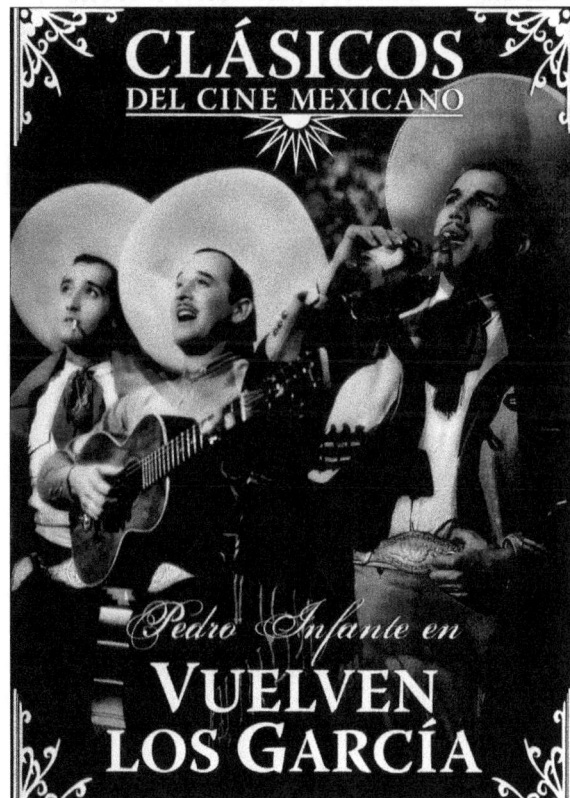

Language Points

- line **2**: *Cielito lindo* literally means "pretty little heaven". Endearments of this kind resist accurate translation.

- line **10**: *se lo*. The indirect object pronoun would normally be *le* but it changes to *se* if it is followed by a direct object pronoun (*lo*).

- line **14**: *encuentra* (from *encontrar,* to find).

Endearments In Spanish

Amorcito — My Little Love

Cariño — 'Darling' (Literally: affection)

Mi Vida — My Life

Mi Sol — My Sun

Mi Tesoro — My Treasure

Corazón — (My) Heart

Mi Cielo - My Heaven

Muñequita - Little Doll

Belleza — Beautiful

Princesa — Princess

Dulzura — Sweetness

Querido — (My) Loved One

Lucero — Bright Star

Florecita — Little Flower

Mi Reina — My Queen

Mi Rey — My King

Corazoncito — My Heart / Little Heart

Mi Hombre Hermoso — My Handsome Man.

A very useful phrase: Te ves bien — You Look Good.

Te ves bonita — You look pretty.

6.
Angelitos negros

Lyrics: Andrés Blanco, Venezuela, 1948;
music: Manuel Álvarez Maciste

Artist: Vicente Fernández

Andrés Blanco

1. **Pintor, nacido en mi tierra**
   Painter, born in my country

2. **con el pincel extranjero,**
   With the foreign paint brush,

3. **pintor, que sigues el rumbo**
   painter who follows the direction

4. **de tantos pintores viejos,**
   of so many old painters,

5. **aunque la Virgen sea blanca**
   although the Virgin (Mary) be white

6. **píntame Angelitos negros**
   Paint for me little black angels

7. **que también se van al cielo**
   Because they too go to heaven

8. **todos los negritos buenos.**
   all good little blacks.

9. **Pintor, si pintas con amor**
   Painter, if you paint with love

10. **¿por qué desprecias su color**
    Why do you scorn their color

11. **si sabes que en el cielo**
    If you know that in heaven

12. **también nos quiere Dios?**
    God loves us too.

13. **Pintor de santos, de alcobas*,**
    Painter of saints and bedrooms

14. **si tienes alma en el cuerpo,**
    If you have a soul in your body

15. **¿por qué al pintar tus cuadros**
    why, when you were painting your paintings

16. **te olvidaste de los negros?**
    Did you forget the little black ones?

17. **Siempre que pintas iglesias**
    Whenever you paint churches

18. **¡pintas Angelitos negros!**
    you paint little black angels!

19. **¡Pero nunca te acordaste**
    But you never remembered

20. **de pintar ¡un ángel negro!**
    to paint a black angel.

21. **¡Un ángel negro!**
    A black angel!

---

* *Alcobas* in line 13 derives from Arabic. The Arabs controlled Spain for about seven centuries and left their mark in many ways, including language. Some scholars attribute an Arabic origin to 3000-4000 Spanish words. Google "Arab influence on Spanish" and you will find several interesting sites. Look for a beautifully illustrated article by Nada Shaath.

Robert Stuart Thomson

General Notes

Angelitos negros was originally a poem written by Andrés Eloy Blanco, born in Cumana, Venezuela, in 1897. He practiced law, wrote poetry and spent several years in prison for his left-wing tendencies and involvement in anti-regime politics. He died in an automobile accident in Mexico City in 1955. It was only years after Andrés Eloy Blanco wrote *Angelitos negros* that it was set to music by the Mexican Manuel Álvarez Maciste.

Manuel Álvarez Maciste

In 1948 *Angelitos negros* was featured in a movie of the same name starring the Mexican idol Pedro Infante. Pedro plays a famous Mexican singer (not himself) who falls in love with a beautiful blonde, woos and marries her. The blonde does not know who her mother was or that her real mother was black. Her mother, eager to give her every advantage in life, hides the information from her with the best of motives. When the blonde has her first child it turns out to be a mulatto. She does not accept the kid and behaves coldly towards her. I won't give the plot away. Suffice it to say that Pedro is well aware of the whole situation and tries to make up for the child's lack of maternal love. *Angelitos negros* is a song that he sings to his daughter when, about age three, she receives her first dose of rejection by her peers at her own birthday party. Pedro sings it beautifully but don't miss Vicente Fernández version on Youtube. I bought this movie in Mexico and play it from time to time to review my Spanish.

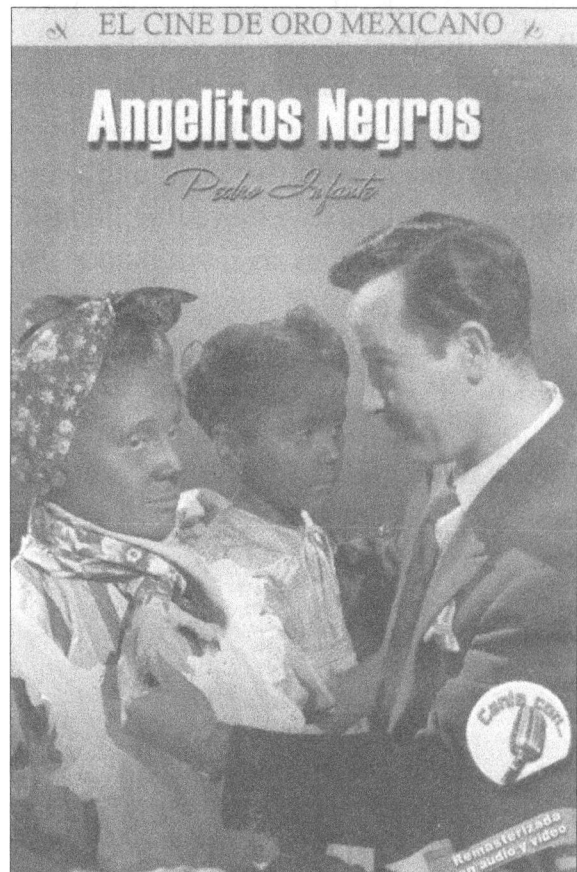

EL CINE DE ORO MEXICANO

Angelitos Negros

Pedro Infante

About 1986 I became infatuated with the beauty of songs in Spanish and in that year I took a cruise which stopped for the day in Puerto Caldera in Costa Rica. Rather than go by bus to visit the capital, San José, I chose to spend the day in a small village on the coast. My intention was to connect with the locals and practice my Spanish. To achieve this I would try to engage them in conversation by asking for help: could they please explain why *alcobas* is mentioned in line **13** of *Angelitos negros*. The grocer (shop number one) didn't know but he insisted on taking me to the pharmacist (who would surely know). No luck there so the grocer, the pharmacist and I went to consult the baker. And on it went, to other shops. In brief, we (myself and about ten local people) ended up, several hours later, in the shop of a guitar maker. He solved the riddle and proceeded to sing *Angelitos negros* for us. ¡Ay, qué rico! What a fascinating day it turned out to be! And it taught me that the best way to get talking Spanish with strangers in Latin countries is to approach them with a polite, "Perdón. Tengo un problema. Tal vez usted me puede ayudar." *(Maybe you can help me.)* Try it — it works.

Language Points

- line **6**: *píntame* (paint for me): imperative.

- line **13**: *alcobas* (bedrooms) refers to the custom in Latin countries of putting religious pictures on the walls of one's bedroom.

- line **16**: *te olvidaste*, reflexive verb *(olvidarse)* in the preterite (simple past) tense.

- line **19**: *te acordaste*, reflexive verb *(acordarse)* in the preterite. *Angelitos* in line **6** and *negritos* in line **8** are affectionate diminutives.

7.
Siboney

Ernesto Lecuona, Cuba, 1928

Artist: Plácido Domingo

Ernesto Lecuona

1. Siboney, yo te quiero, yo me muero por tu amor.
Siboney, I love you, I am dying for your love.

2. Siboney, en tu boca la miel puso su dulzor.
Siboney, in your mouth honey placed its sweetness.

3. Ven a mí que te quiero y que todo tesoro eres tu para mí.
Come to me who love you and a complete treasure you are for me

4. Siboney, al arrullo de la palma pienso en ti.
Siboney, with the soothing sound of the palm tree I think of you.

5. Siboney de mis sueños si no oyes la queja de mi voz…
Siboney of my dreams, if you don't hear the lament of my voice…

6. Siboney, si no vienes me moriré de amor.
Siboney, if you don't come I will die of love.

7. Siboney de mis sueños te espero con ansia en mi caney
Siboney of my dreams, I await you with anxiousness in my hut

8. porque tu eres el sueño de mi amor, Siboney.
because you are the mistress of my love.

9. Siboney, oye el eco de mi canto de cristal.
Siboney, hear the echo of my crystalline song.

Repeat 7-9.

10. No te pierdas por entre el rudo manigual.
Don't get lost in the horrible swamp!

_____

_____

_____

_____

_____

Plácido Domingo

General Notes

Ernesto Lecuona (1895-1963) left a huge musical legacy (See photo.) One of his greatest compositions is "The Andalusian Suite" which contains the famous *Malagueña*. (Words for it were written some time after its composition. Google YouTube to hear it.). Siboney is the name of a small town on the coast of Cuba. The rhythm is bolero/rumba which complements a soaring, emotional melody.

Plácido Domingo was born in Mexico City in 1941 and spent most of his youth there. His parents were zarzuela singers from Spain and from an early age Plácido was exposed to popular music. Maybe this partly accounts for the ease with which he has been able to interpret popular music, including love songs. Plácido has had a remarkable career as an operatic tenor of the first magnitude, covering roles from Verdi to Wagner. I hear he has plans to open a restaurant in New York City. That will be an interesting place to visit. I hope he will sing there.

Listen for the key change from line four to line five and you will appreciate how it intensifies the emotional impact of the music.

Language Points

- line **10**: *te pierdas* (from *perderse*): reflexive verb in the imperative mood.

Notes

8.
Cucurrucucú, paloma

Tomás Méndez, Mexico, 1927

Artist: Lola Beltrán

Lola Beltrán

1. **Dicen que por las noches**
   They say that at night

2. **nomás se le iba en puro llorar.**
   All he did was cry all the time.

3. **Dicen que no comía**
   They say that he didn't eat,

4. **nomás se le iba en puro tomar.**
   All he did was drink.

5. **Juran que el mismo cielo**
   They swear that Heaven itself

6. **se estremecía al oír su llanto,**
   rumbled upon hearing his crying,

7. **cómo sufrió por ella**
   how he suffered for her

8. **y hasta en su muerte la fue llamando.**
   and even when he was dying he kept on calling for her.

9. **¡Ay, ay, ay, ay, ay! lloraba.**
   Ay, ay, ay, ay, ay! he sobbed.

10. **¡Ay, ay, ay, ay, ay! gemía**
    Ay, ay, ay, he groaned!

11. **¡Ay, ay, ay, ay, ay! cantaba.**
    Ay, ay, ay, he sang!

12. **¡De pasión mortal moría!**
    From mortal passion he was dying!

13. **Que una paloma triste**
    If a sad dove

14. **muy de mañana le va a cantar**
    very early in the morning starts singing to you,

15. **a la casita sola**
    alone in her little house

16. **con sus puertitas de par en par.**
    with its little doors wide open

17. **Juran que esa paloma**
    They swear that that dove

18. **no es otra cosa más que su alma**
    Is nothing other than his soul

19. **que todavía espera**
    which is still waiting

20. **a que regrese la desdichada.**
    for the luckless girl to come back.

21. **¡Cucurrucucú, paloma! ¡Cucurrucucú, no llores!**
    Cucurrucucu, dove! Cucurrucucu, don't cry!

22. **Las piedras, jamás, paloma,**
    The stones, never, dove,

23. **¿qué van a saber de amores?**
    What are they going to know about love(s)?

24. **¡Cucurrucucú! Paloma, ¡no llores!**
    Cucurrucucu, dove! Don't cry!

Tomás Méndez

General Notes

Tomás Méndez was born on July 25, 1927, in Fresnillo, Zacatecas (Mexico) and died in 1995. Two other classics which he wrote are *Paloma negra* and *Puñalada trapera*.

Language Points

- line **6**: *píntame* (paint for me): imperative in the present tense.

- lines **2, 4**: *se le iba en puro llorar*. This is an idiom which means "All he did was cry."

The same goes for line 4: *se le iba en puro tomar* (all he did was drink). It is difficult if not impossible to explain idioms grammatically. Maybe it's best not to try—one just has to learn them.

- line **3**: *comía*: imperfect tense of *comer*, to eat. This song contains several verbs in the imperfect tense: *se estremecía* (from *estremecerse*, to take pity on), in line six. Others: *cantaba* (line **9**); *gemía* (line **10**), *moría* (line **12**).

- line **19-20**: *espera a que regrese la desdichada* (waits until the luckless creature returns).

The *espera* in the first clause must be followed by a verb in the subjunctive (*regrese*) because the outcome is uncertain.

Winston Churchill's family motto was *Fiel pero desdichada*. i.e. faithful but unlucky.

- lines **22-23**: Dove, stones will never know about love, i.e. you might have suffered but better that than to have lived life as unfeeling as a stone. *Las piedras* is a good metaphor for something which is completely insensitive and without feeling. Shakespeare uses it in *Julius Caesar*: "You blocks! You stones! You worse than senseless things." (spoken by a senator addressing the huge crowd who are waiting to greet Caesar after his victory over Pompey). For a similar thought about insensitivity see song 19 (*Hey!*), verses 10-11.

Lola Beltrán ("*Lola La Grande*")

In my opinion, the greatest interpreter of *Cucurrucucú, paloma* is Lola Beltrán or "Lola la Grande" as Mexicans call her. She was born in Rosario, Sinaloa in 1932, moved to Mexico City in her early 20s to work as a secretary but soon made the right connections and started singing in clubs. She recorded many songs and appeared in about thirty movies. She also had her own television shows: *El studio de Lola Beltrán* and *Noches tapatías*. Upon her death in 1996 her body lay in state in the rotunda of the Palacio de Bella Artes in Mexico City, an honor accorded to few. Recently (March, 2015) I asked my top-notch dentist in Puerto Vallarta for her opinion of Lola. Her reply: "¡Es lo máximo!" That reaction is typical, at least of the older generations. A movie based on Lola's life, *Cucurrucucú, paloma*, appeared in 1965. See YouTube for more songs by her.

9.
Historia de un amor

Carlos Almarán, Panamá 1956
Artists: Eydie Gorme and the Trio los Panchos

VERSE ONE

1. Ya no estás más a mi lado, corazón.
You are no longer at my side, dear one.

2. En el alma solo tengo soledad
In my heart all I have is solitude.

3. y si ya no puedo verte
And if I cannot see you

4. ¿por qué Dios me hizo quererte
Why did God make me love you

5. para hacerme sufrir más?
to make me suffer more?

VERSE TWO

6. Siempre fuiste la razón de mi existir,
You always were the reason for my existence

7. adorarte para mí fue religión
Adoring you for me was a religion

8. y en tus besos yo encontraba
And in your kisses I found

9. el calor que me brindaba
the warmth that offered to me

10. el amor y la pasión.
love and passion

(9-10: i.e. the warmth that love and passion offered me.)

CHORUS

11. Es la historia de un amor
It is the story of a love

12. como no hay otro igual
like none other

13. que me hizo comprender
which made me understand

14. todo el bien, todo el mal,
all good and all evil.

15. que le dio luz a mi vida,
Which gave light to my life,

16. apagándola después.
extinguishing it afterwards.

17. ¡Ay! ¡Qué vida tan oscura!
Oh, what a gloomy life!

18. ¡Sin tu amor no viviré!
Without your love I will not live.

Repeat 11-18

19. Es la historia de un amor.

General Notes

As we saw in song 2 (*¡Amor! ¡amor!*) the Christian images (*alma, Dios, sufrir, religión, pasión, bien y mal, luz*) abound here as well. As usual, culture is embedded in the language.

Carlos Eleta Almarán (1918-2013)

The composer of this song is Carlos Eleta Almarán who apparently wrote it in sympathy for his brother who had lost his wife just days before. *Historia de un amor* is featured in a Mexican movie of the same name which came out in 1956.

Language Points

In this song the nouns and verbs dominate; there are very few adjectives or adverbs. This gives the writing clarity, concision and power.

The Historical Origins of Love Songs

Not surprisingly, the language and imagery of these modern love songs have antecedents and if we look for them we are taken far back in Spanish history. The most impressive period of early lyric poetry is Spain's *Siglo de Oro* (Golden Age). From the examples below you can see continuity from the 16th century to the present day, both in the attitudes towards love and in the imagery used to describe it. The anonymous poet below sounds almost like Agustín Lara in *Noche de ronda* (song no. 3, above).

"Luna que reluces,
Oh moon who shines

toda la noche alumbres.
All night may you illuminate.

Ay, luna que reluces
Oh, moon who shines

blanca y plateada
White and silvery

toda la noche alumbres
All night may you shine on

a mi linda enamorada.
My beautiful loved one.

Amada que reluces
Oh loved one who shines

toda la noche alumbres."
All night may you shine on.

(Anonymous, ca 1550)

The following verses by Garcilaso de la Vega were probably written about 1530. The sentiment expressed in them–the suffering caused by unrequited love–is the same that surfaces centuries later in such songs as *Miraron llorar a este hombre* (song 12), *Se me olvidó otra vez* (song 14) and *¡Hey!* (song 19).

O, más dura que mármol a mis quejas,
Oh, harder than marble to my laments

y al encendido fuego en que me quemo,
And to the fire in which I burn myself

más helada que nieve, Galatea!
Colder than snow (you are), Galatea!

Estoy muriendo y aun la vida temo:
I am dying and even life I fear:
I am dying and I fear even life:

témola con razón, pues tú me dejas.
I fear it with reason since you are leaving me.

The illustrations show three of the greatest writers of Spain's Golden Age (*Siglo de Oro*): Lope de Vega, Calderón de la Barca and Cervantes.

Other tendencies which seem to have filtered down to modern times from the *Siglo de Oro* are pride, hypersensitivity to insults, and a tendency to idealize the person loved and to decribe her with religious or even mystical language.

Lope de Vega

Calderón de la Barca

Cervantes

10.
Sabor a mí

Álvaro Carrillo Alarcón, Mexico, 1959

Artists: Eydie Gorme and the Trío los Panchos

Álvaro Carrillo Alarcón

1. Tanto tiempo disfrutamos de este amor,
For so long we enjoyed this love,

2. nuestras almas se acercaron tanto así
our souls came so close this way

3. que yo guardo tu sabor
that I keep (still have) your taste

4. pero tú llevas también sabor a mí.
but you too carry my taste with you.

5. Si negaras mi presencia en tu vivir
If you were to deny my presence in your life

6. bastaría con abrazarte y conversar.
it would be sufficient to embrace you and converse (with you).

7. Tanta vida yo te di
I gave you so much life

8. Que por fuerza tienes ya sabor a mí.
that perforce you still have my taste.

CHORUS

9. No pretendo ser tu dueña/o.
I don't claim to be your owner.

10. No soy nada y no tengo vanidad.
I am nothing and I have no vanity.

11. De mi vida doy lo bueno.
of my life I give the best.

12. Soy tan pobre—¿qué otra cosa puedo dar?
I am so poor--what else can I give

13. Pasarán más de mil años, muchos más ;
A thousand years will go by, many more:

14. yo no sé si tenga amor la eternidad
I don't know if there is love in eternity

15. pero allá tal como aquí en la boca
But there, just like here, in your mouth

16 llevarás sabor a mí, sabor a mí.
you will carry my taste with you.

Repeat verses 9-16

General Notes

Álvaro Carrillo Alarcón was born in San Juan Cacahuatepec, Oaxaca in 1921. He took a degree in agricultural engineering in 1945 but within a few years abandoned this career to devote himself to musical composition. He wrote over 300 songs. In 1969 he and his wife were killed in a tragic head-on collision on the highway between Cuernavaca and Mexico City. Every October the University of Chapingo hosts a *festival de la canción* in Carrillo's honor. A movie, *Sabor a mí* was made about his life.

The intercultural chasm between the United States and Mexico which Alan Riding wrote about in his *Distant Neighbors* (1984) was made even deeper by the distorted image of Mexico as conveyed in American versions of Mexican love songs. The lines quoted below (from *Be true to me*) are trite and unimaginative and give a poor idea of the beauty and depth of the Latin originals.

Be true to me
(American version of *Sabor a mí*).

If I prove how much I love you with each kiss
Will you cross your heart and promise me all this,
That it's more than just a thrill
That you love me and you will
Be true to me.
I will give you all my love, Dear, here and now
If you'll only make this solemn little vow:
That you mean just what you say.
Please be fair in every way,
Be true to me.
I'm so helpless when you touch me,
Feeling feelings that I never felt before.
Oh, my darling, say you'll love me. (etc. etc.)

Language Points

- line **3**: *Gusto* is the faculty of taste; *sabor* is the flavor of what is tasted. When you buy ice cream you have a choice of *sabores*. Here is my *Diccionario avanzado's* definition of *sabor*: *calidad de una sustancia que se percibe por el sentido de gusto* (taste).

- line **9**: *pretendo* and the English word "pretend" are deceptive cognates (or "false friends"), i.e. words which have the same origin but through the years have taken on different meanings.

Notes

11.
Caminito

Peñaloza and Filiberto, Argentina, 1925

Artist: Carlos Gardel

VERSE ONE

1. **Caminito que el tiempo ha borrado**
Little path which time has erased

2. **que juntos un día nos viste pasar,**
Which one day saw us pass by together,

3. **he venido por última vez,**
I have come for the last time.

4. **he venido a contarte mi mal.**
I have come to tell you about my misfortune.

5. **Caminito que entonces estabas**
Little path who used to be

6. **bordado de trébol y juncos en flor,**
Lined with clover and flowering rushes,

7. **una sombra ya pronto serás,**
A shadow you will soon be

8. **una sombra lo mismo que yo.**
A shadow the same as me.

CHORUS

9. **Desde que se fue, triste vivo yo.**
Since she left I live sadly.

10. **Caminito amigo, yo también me voy.**
Little path, my friend, I too am leaving.

11. **Desde que se fue, nunca más volvió.**
Since she went, she never returned.

12. **Seguiré sus pasos.**
I will follow her steps

13. **Caminito, ¡adiós!**
Little path, adiós!

VERSE TWO

14. **Caminito que todas las tardes**
Little path (on) which every afternoon

15. **feliz recorría cantando mi amor,**
Happy, I walked, singing of my love.

16. **no le digas si vuelve a pasar**
Don't tell her if she passes by again

17. **que mi llanto tu huella regó.**
That my tears sprinkled your traces.

18. **Caminito cubierto de cardos**
Little path covered with thistles

19. la mano del tiempo tu huella borró.

The hand of time has erased your traces.

20. Yo a tu lado quisiera caer,

I would like to fall at your side

21. y que el tiempo nos mate a los dos.

And may time kill both of us.

CHORUS

22. Desde que se fue, triste vivo yo.

Since she left, I live in sadness.

23. Caminito amigo, yo también me voy.

Caminito, my friend, I too am leaving.

24. Desde que se fue, nunca más volvió.

Since she left, she never returned.

25. Seguiré sus pasos. Caminito, ¡adiós!

I will follow her steps. Caminito, farewell!

General Points

Plácido Domingo sang *Caminito* in the 1990 Three Tenors Concert in Rome. Look it up on YouTube.

Caminito brings to mind in several ways *Le Lac* (1820) by Alfonse de Lamartine and it is quite possible that Peñaloza knew the poem which is widely considered a masterpiece of the Romantic era in France. In *Le Lac* the narrator returns to the lake where he and his love (now dead) used to walk and enjoy the love which they shared. He reflects on her, his great loss and the shortness of life. Both poems use personification in similar ways. Here are a few lines from Lamartine's poem.

Ainsi, toujours poussés vers de nouveaux rivages,

Dans la nuit éternelle emportés sans retour,

Ne pourrons-nous jamais sur l'océan des âges

Jeter l'ancre un seul jour?

Ô lac! L'année à peine a fini sa carrière

Et près des flots chéris qu'elle devait revoir,

Regarde! Je viens seul m'asseoir sur cette pierre

Où tu la vis s'asseoir.

It goes as follows in a free but good English version:

Thus driven forth forever to new shores

Borne towards Eternal Night and never away,

Sailing the Sea of Ages, can we not

Drop anchor for one day?

Oh, Lake! The year has scarcely spun its course.

Now, by the waves she should have seen again,
Watch how I sit, alone, upon this stone
On which you saw her then.

Lamartine thought that sadness was the most natural emotion of lyric poetry (including songs): "Le chant naturel de l'homme est triste." (The natural song of man is a sad one.) Would you agree? It seems to me that many of the songs in *Love Songs in Spanish for Enjoyment and Learning* (especially those dealing with unrequited love) fall into the category of sadness.

Alphonse de Lamartine (1790-1869)

Language Points

- lines **5-6** When he walked this trail with his love, nature was alive and flourishing; when she has gone and he returns, alone, nature is in winter mode and seems dead. Nature is presented as an empathizing witness.

- lines **1, 5, 10, 13** etc. The word *caminito* is repeated throughout the song, driving home through its repetition the themes of obsession and lost love.

Gardel drops a number of final s's and z's: *vez* (line **3**); *serás* (line **7**); *pasos* (line **12**); *adiós* (lines **13** and **25**). This is common in Argentina.

This well-developed song makes a good review of verb tenses because it contains such a wide range of them: preterite, compound past (traditionally known as "the present perfect"), imperfect (or "descriptive past"), future, conditional, and present (including the imperative and subjunctive moods).

present — line **10**: *me voy*
preterite — line **2**: *viste*; line **9**: *se fue*; line **17**: *regó*
imperfect — line **5**: *estabas*; line **15**: *recorría*
future — line **7**: *serás*; line **23**: *seguiré*
conditional — line **20**: *quisiera*

There is also an imperative (line **16**: *No le digas*) and a subjunctive (line **21**: *mate).* This proliferation of verbs in several tenses gives the song a dynamic, fluid quality, well suited to the Argentine tango.

The Strange Story of *Caminito*

Caminito has a strange history. The words were written by Gabino Coria Peñaloza in 1903 and tell the story of his first love, a young school teacher he met and wooed in the foothills of the Andes at Olta, in Argentina's La Rioja province Their favorite promenade was an out-of-the way path in the wilds. Unfortunately he had to leave the area for a year and while absent her parents sold their house and took her with them. There is some speculation that she had gotten pregnant, but whatever the case, Peñaloza lost her and from this tender and bitter experience he forged a poem called *Caminito.*

Meanwhile, Oscar de Dios Filiberto, born in 1885 in Buenos Aires, discovered a lovely tango melody one day as he was out walking in the streets of a poor section of Buenos Aires. The year was 1924. About a year later Filiberto was introduced to Peñaloza at a party given by Quinquela Martín, who became a famous painter/champion of the working class (and much admired by Mussolini). Filiberto asked Peñaloza if he would write the words to the fine tango music that he had written. Peñaloza listened to the music once then replied that he didn't need to write it because he had already written it, way back in 1903.

Filiberto   Peñaloza

Thus did *Caminito* come to be. It is remarkable how well the music and the lyrics go together. The use of what John Ruskin called "the pathetic fallacy", i.e. where the poet talks to an inanimate object as if it had feelings and intelligence, works well in this tango. Nostalgia in all its forms is a common theme in tangos.

Carlos Gardel
(1890-1935)

Carlos Gardel, the famous tango singer and composer, lost no time in adding this beautiful song to his repertoire. It has been said that the three best-known tangos ever written are *La cumparsita, El choclo* (which became *Kiss of Fire* when adapted to the North American market) and *Caminito.*

Some songs have a story and it is interesting to find out what it is. Here again the Internet is handy, cheap, and full of information.

Notes

12.
Miraron llorar a este hombre

Homero Aguilas Cabrera, Mexico, 1979
Artist: Vicente Fernández

A sculpture on the Malecón, Puerto Vallarta

1. "¿Qué caso tiene buscarla?
¿Qué caso tiene seguirla?
What's the point in looking for
her? What's the point in following
her?

2. De nada vale adorarla si no
podré conseguirla."
It's worth nothing to adore her if I
won't be able to get her.

3. Así me dije una noche,
mojándome en una esquina.
Thus I said to myself one night,
getting soaked (or weeping?) on a
street corner.

4. Después me di media vuelta.
Tomé por cualquier camino.
Then I turned around. I took any
old road.

5. Quería salir por la puerta que
me abre un vaso de vino.
I wanted to go out the door that a
glass of wine opens for me.

6. Quería arrancarla de mi alma,
¡mandarla por dónde vino!
I wanted to tear her out of my
soul, send her to where she came
from.

7. El vino agrandó mi pena, la
pena sacó mi llanto,
The wine increased my pain, the
pain drew forth my tears,

8. el llanto me abrió la boca, mi
boca dijo su nombre.
The tears opened my mouth, my
mouth said her name.

9. Y allí entre copa tras copa,
miraron llorar a este hombre.
And there, between one cup after
another, they watched this man
cry.

Repeat from 4 to 9.

General Notes

As I walked through the streets of Puerto Vallarta one night I heard loud ranchera music coming from the second story of a building. It was Vicente Fernández singing (via stereo) *Miraron llorar a este hombre,* a clever song which explores the strange mystery of wine's power, the crazy quixotic business of continuing to love someone who doesn't reciprocate your love, and the thoughts of revenge which are fueled by drink. All of this is developed imaginatively in few words.

Vicente Fernández recorded a vast number of songs. One of the most poignant, in my opinion, is *Se vende un caballo* (Horse for Sale). It too gives insight into Mexican ranchero culture. Here are the first few lines:

Puse un letrero en mi rancho, cuando lo estaba clavando, sentí ganas de llorar.
I put up a sign on my ranch (and) when I was nailing it up I felt like crying.

Dice se vende caballo, mi penco estaba en un lado, y comenzó a relinchar
It says horse for sale (and) my nag stood to the side and began to whinny

como si hubiera leído, como si hubiera entendido que yo lo quería vender.
As if it had read, as if it had understood that I wanted to sell it.

Try Youtubing "Vicente Fernández and Se vende un caballo." You can even hear the horse whinnying in the background. I never cease to be amazed by the creative imagination of the Mexican/Latin-American mind.

Learning songs like *Miraron* increases your knowledge of Spanish and gives you insight into the Mexican mind (or at least the mind of some Mexicans). *Arrancar* (meaning to tear out by the roots) is violent and is a tip-off that underneath the stoical exterior of some Mexican men there might lie a volcano. *Las apariencias engañan.* (Appearances are deceiving, as the Spanish saying goes.) One's emotions are to be kept hidden. A "real man" can't be seen crying in public! ¡Caramba! What will people think?

Language Points

Title: *Miraron llorar a este hombre*: They watched this man cry.

This song shows the preterite (simple past) used effectively: *dije, di, tome, agrandó, sacó, abrió, dijo, miraron.* There are also some idioms: *qué caso tiene, mojar,* and *esquina.*

The proliferation of verbs in the preterite and the imperfect make this song an excellent exercise in those verb tenses.

Vicente Fernández

For me the best interpreter of this song is Vicente Fernández, who was born in 1940 in Huentitán el Alto, Jalisco into an impoverished ranchero family. For economic reasons he had to quit school in grade five and went to work, waiting tables, etc. At age fourteen he placed first in an amateur singing contest in Guadalajara and found his calling, picking up lots of on-site training by singing in restaurants and night clubs. His big break came in 1966 when he was hired by CBS Mexico. This led to recording and movie contracts. His 1974 movie, *La ley del monte* was a huge hit. They made a movie about his life: *Historia de un ídolo.* As I write this (March 2015) beside a swimming pool in Puerto Vallarta I have to tell you that since I started dying my moustache black I have had five Mexican strangers in the past month alone ask me if I was Vicente Fernández or at least his brother. No, Señor! But I wish!

13.
Piel canela

Roberto Capo, Puerto Rico, 1953

Artist: Roberto (Bobby) Capo

San Juan, Puerto Rico

1. **Que se quede el infinito sin estrellas**
   Let the heavens remain without stars

2. **y que pierda el ancho mar su inmensidad**
   And let the broad sea lose its immensity

3. **pero el negro de tus ojos que no muera**
   but let it not die, the darkness of your eyes

4. **y el canela de tu piel se quede igual.**
   And the cinnamon color of your skin, let it remain the same.

5. **Si perdiera el arco iris su belleza**
   If the rainbow were to lose its beauty

6. **y las flores su perfume y su color**
   And the flowers (lost) their perfume and their color

7. **no sería tan inmensa mi tristeza**
   My sadness would not be so immense

8. **como aquella de quedarme sin tu amor.**
   As that (sadness) of being left without your love.

CHORUS

9. **Me importas tú, y tú, y tú**
   You matter to me

10. **y solamente tú, y tú, y tú.**
    And only you.

11. **Me importas tú, y tú, y tú**
    You matter to me,

12. **y nadie más que tú.**
    And no one more than you.

13. **Ojos negros, piel canela**
    Dark eyes, cinnamon skin

14. **que me llegan a desesperar,**
    Which lead me to despair,

Repeat lines 9-12; 9-14; 9-12.

BOBBY CAPO

Epoca de Oro

General Notes

The images from nature are conspicuous in this song: *infinito, las estrellas, el mar, el arco iris, las flores*. *Piel canela* is from Puerto Rico, that island of balmy weather where they spend so much time outdoors, close to nature. It is not surprising that a Puerto Rican song would reflect much of nature's bounty. As usual, language reflects culture. This gem of a song was composed by Roberto Capo (1922-1989). From line nine on this song is pure cha-cha-cha.

Language Points

This song would make an excellent exercise on the subjunctive.

- lines **1-4**: The subjunctives here (*se quede, pierda, muera, se quede*) all convey the idea of a wish.

- line **5**: *perdiera* is the imperfect subjunctive of *perder* and must be used here because there is a hypothetical or contrary-to-fact situation. A past subjunctive is also implied in line 6 and its subject is *las flores*.

The Caney Group. Bobby is fourth from the left.

Notes

14.
¿Y qué hiciste del amor que me juraste?

Mario de Jesús Báez, Dominican Republic

Artist: Javier Solís

Javier Solís

1. ¿Y qué hiciste del amor que me juraste?
And what have you done with the love that you swore to me?

2. ¿Y qué has hecho de los besos que te di?
And what have you done with the kisses that I gave you?

3. ¿Y qué excusa puedes darme si faltaste
And what excuse can you give me if you were unfaithful

4. y mataste la esperanza que hubo en mí?
And killed the hope that once existed in me?

5. ¡Y qué ingrato es el destino que me hiere!
And how ungrateful is the destiny that wounds me!

6. ¡Y qué absurda la razón de mi pasión!
And how absurd is the reason for my passion!

7. ¡Y qué necio es este amor que no se muere
And how foolish is this love which doesn't die.

8. y prefiere perdonarte tú traición!
And prefers to forgive (you) your betrayal!

9. Y pensar que en mi vida fuiste flama
And to think that, in my life, you were a flame

10. y el caudal de mi gloria fuiste tú
And that the high point of my glory was you

11. y llegué a quererte con el alma
And I reached the point of loving you with my soul

12. y hoy me mata de tristeza tu actitud.
And today kills me with sadness your attitude (and today your attitude kills me with sadness.)

13. ¿Y a qué debo, dime, entonces, tu abandono?
And to what do I owe, tell me then, your abandonment?

14. ¿Y en qué ruta tú promesa se perdió?
And on what road did your promise get lost?

15. Y si dices la verdad yo te perdono
And if you tell the truth I will forgive you

16. y te llevo en mi recuerdo junto a Dios.
And I will carry you in my memory in a place next to God.

Repeat lines 9-16.

Robert Stuart Thomson

Mario de Jesús Báez

General Notes

Mario de Jesús Báez was born in San Pedro de Macorís (in the Dominican Republic) in 1924. He moved to New York City in 1945 and took his first music lessons there. In 1959 he moved to Mexico City where he lived until his death in July, 2016.

Javier Solís (his real name is Gabriel Siria Levario) was born on September 1, 1931 in Nogales (Sonora) Mexico. His early life was marked by poverty and he dropped out of school at the age of ten. A lucky break came at eighteen when his talent was recognized and encouraged by the Trio los Panchos who arranged for him to record an album for CBC. One of his biggest hits was the lovely *Amanecí entre tus brazos* which is well worth googling if you don't know of it. Solís also appeared in over twenty movies but he is best remembered as a singer, one of the "Tres Gallos" (three roosters), the others being Pedro Infante and Jorge Negrete. In Spanish "gallos" connotes both singing (including cockadoodledooing) and physical bravery. In 1966 Solís came to an untimely

end: after a gallbladder operation fatal complications set in.

It takes a master craftsman to write a song in which every line begins with the same word and not bore the listener to death.

Lines one to eight contain angry, bitter reproaches, both of the girl and of destiny. The tone changes dramatically in lines nine to eleven when the singer celebrates the joy that her love once brought him. As I mentioned earlier (p. 9) in connection with Spanish lyrics, religious (even mystical) language is sometimes used to describe man-woman love: words like *esperanza* (line 4), *pasión* (line 6), *perdonar* (line 8), *flama* (line 9), *gloria* (line 10), *alma* (line 11), and *Dios* (line 16). Spiritual words such as these add power and depth of feeling to the song.

The change from major to minor key in line nine conveys musically the shift from reproaches (1-8) to thoughts of the love that once was.

Two American songs which comment on the absurdity of passionate love are *Stupid Cupid* and *Something Stupid Like I Love You*.

Language Points

This song would make a good lesson on the preterite tense.

Be sure to google "¿Y qué hiciste?" and Luis Miguel for a passionate contemporary interpretation of this song.

Notes

15.
Di que no es verdad

Alberto Domínguez, Mexico (1939-?)

Artists: Trío los Panchos

Trío los Panchos

1. **Con el alma llena de amargura y sin saber qué hacer**
With the soul full of bitterness and without knowing what to do

2. **he venido aquí con esta duda a escuchar tu voz.**
I have come here with this doubt to listen to your voice.

3. **Di que no es verdad lo que murmuran de los dos.**
Say that it's not true what they are muttering about the two of us.

4. **Di que no es verdad que has dejado a mi amor.**
Say it isn't true that you have stopped loving me.

5. **Di que no es verdad, que es envidia o maldad**
Say it isn't true, that it's (the) envy or malice

6. **de alguien que quiere robar tu corazón.**
Of someone who wants to steal your heart.

7. **No podrán jamás a nuestras almas separar.**
They will never be able to separate our souls.

8. **No podrán jamás nuestro amor profanar.**
They will never be able to desecrate our love.

9. **Habla, por favor, ya por bien ya por mal,**
Speak, please, whether for good or for bad,
(Speak, please, whether the news is good or bad.)

10. **para poder sonreír o llorar.**
In order to be able to smile or cry.
(So that I will know whether to smile or cry.)

Repeat verses 9-10

_____

_____

_____

_____

Robert Stuart Thomson

General Notes

The Trío Los Panchos is famous for its rich, delicate sound, admirably suited to smooth ballads and boleros. Los Panchos started out in the 1940s and reached their pinnacle of success in the 1960s when they collaborated brilliantly with Eydie Gorme, lending rich harmonies and Mexican color to her recordings (see notes to song 2). The records they made with Eydie became best sellers. Los Panchos achieved their attractive sound partly by introducing the *requinto*, a smaller, higher pitched version of the standard acoustic guitar. Another distinctive feature of Los Panchos was that all members could sing and play virtuoso guitar.

Language Points

- line 4: *has dejado a mi amor. Has dejado* here means "you have abandoned."

- line **13**: *No podrán jamás nuestro amor profanar.* The underlying meaning of this is something like "They will never be able to cheapen our love by pulling it down to their level."

Profanar could be translated by *profane* (used as a verb) as in Romeo's remark to Juliet when he first takes her hand at the Capulets' party:

If I profane with my unworthiest hand
This holy shrine, the gentle sin is this:
My lips, two blushing pilgrims, ready stand
To smooth that rough touch with a tender kiss.

"This" in verse two refers to what goes before i.e. profaning with his hand.

In *Di que no es verdad* it is suggested that no matter how hard the gossips try, they will never succeed in cheapening the nature of the lovers' feelings for each other. *Historia de un amor* (song 9) also develops the idea of the holiness of the highest kind of human love.

Notes

16.
Se me olvidó otra vez

Juan Gabriel, Mexico, 1974

Artist: Lola Beltrán

Lola Beltrán

1. Probablemente ya de mí te has olvidado
Probably you have already forgotten me

2. y mientras tanto yo te seguiré esperando.
And in the meantime I will keep on waiting for you.

3. No me he querido ir para ver si algún día
I haven't wanted to leave to see if some day

4. que tú quieras volver me encuentres todavía.
that you might want to come back you might still find me.

5. Por eso aún estoy en el lugar de siempre
For that (reason) I am still in the same old place

6. en la misma ciudad y con la misma gente,
In the same city and with the same people,

7. para que tú al volver no encuentres nada extraño
So that on your return you would find nothing different/strange

8. y sea como ayer y nunca más dejarnos.
And (everything) might be like yesterday and never again would we leave each other.

9. Probablemente estoy pidiendo demasiado:
Probably I am asking for too much:

10. se me olvidaba que ya habíamos terminado,
I was forgetting that we had already broken up,

11. que nunca volverás, que nunca me quisiste.
(I was also forgetting) that you will never come back, (and) that you never loved me.

12. Se me olvidó otra vez que sólo yo te quise.
I had forgotten again that it was only me who had loved you

Repeat 5-12.

General Notes

Juan Gabriel was born Alberto Aguilera Valadez on January 7, 1950 in Parácuaro, Mexico. At a very early age he moved with his mother and siblings to Ciudad Juárez in Chihuahua. His youth was unsettled and he lived in and out of orphanages and boarding schools. He became a prolific song writer and won many awards for his songs. Some of his better known compositions are *Hasta que te conocí, Lágrimas y lluvia,* and *Lo pasado, pasado. Se me olvidó* dates from 1974. Unless I miss my guess the sorrow underpinning *Se me olvidó* takes root in the very real experiences of an unusually sensitive person. Such a person I think Gabriel must have been. I am not surprised that he founded an orphanage, "Semjase". Gabriel died of a heart attack in Santa Monica, California in August, 2016.

Here is another passionate song of unrequited love and the longing that it brings with it. The context is Mexico in the 1940s when people tended to stay in the place where they were born, always surrounded by the familiar. The mass exodus of people to the big cities had not yet really started. Between 2009 and 2015 Mexico City grew from 9 million to 21 million. This version of *Se Me Olvidó* is by Lola (La Grande) Beltrán.

Language Points

- line **1**: *te has olvidado de mí* from *olvidarse,* a reflexive verb.

- line **2**: *esperando* from *esperar* (meaning "to wait for"). It also can mean "to hope", which also makes sense here.

- line **3**: *No me he querido ir.* The infinitive is *irse* to leave, go away.

- line **4**: Both *quieras* (from *querer*) and *encuentres* (from *encontrar*) are in the subjunctive mood because it is uncertain if she will return.

- lines **7** and **8**: More subjunctives and more uncertainty: *encuentres* (line **7**, from *encontrar*) and *sea* (line **8**, from *ser*). Lines eight and twelve show how concise Spanish can be.

- line **10** and **11**: *se me olvidaba que* (imperfect or *copretérito* tense) followed by *habíamos terminado* (pluperfect or ante-*copretérito* tense).

In this song the proliferation and variety of the verbs (especially verbs in the subjunctive mood) reflect well the obsessive meanderings of a mind a prey to waiting, uncertainty, and the false expectations caused by his/her own denial.

Notes

17.
Granada

Agustín Lara, Mexico, 1932

Artist: Plácido Domingo

Granada with the Sierra Nevada in the background

INTRODUCTION

1. Granada, tierra soñada por mí,
Granada, land dreamt of by me,

2. mi cantar se vuelve gitano
My song turns into a gypsy

3. cuando es para ti.
when it is for you

4. Mi cantar, hecho de fantasía.
My song, (which is) made of fantasy.

5. Mi cantar, flor de la melancolía
My song, a flower of melancholy

6. que yo te vengo a dar.
That I come to give to you.

VERSE ONE

7. Granada, tierra ensangrentada
Granada, land steeped in blood

8. en tardes de toros,
in afternoons of the corrida,

9. mujer que conserva el embrujo
(Granada is also) a woman who still has the witchcraft

10. de los ojos moros,
of Moorish eyes,

11. te sueño rebelde y gitana,
I dream of you as a rebel and (a) gypsy,

12. cubierta de flores,
covered with flowers,

13 y beso tu boca de grana,
And I kiss your pomegranate-colored mouth,

14. jugosa manzana
a juicy apple

15. que me habla de amores.
that speaks to me of loves.

Moorish architecture in the Nasrid Palace in the Alhambra (Granada, Spain). The word "Alhambra" derives from the Arabic words meaning "the red".

Robert Stuart Thomson

VERSE TWO

16. Granada, manola cantada
Granada, a Manola girl sung

17. en coplas preciosas,
In beautiful couplets,

18. no tengo otra cosa que darte
I have nothing else to give you

19. que un ramo de rosas,
than a bouquet of roses,

20. de rosas de suave fragrancia
of roses of sweet fragrance

21. que le dieran marco a la Virgen Morena.
that they could serve as a (picture) frame for the dark-skinned Virgin.

22. Granada, tu tierra está llena
Granada, your land is full

23. de lindas mujeres, de sangre y de sol.
Of pretty women, blood, and sun.

Repeat: 20-23

Agustín Lara

General Notes

In this song Lara pays homage to the Spanish side of Mexican identity, specifically the beauty and rich history of the ancient city of Granada in Andalusia. From verse seven on he uses a kind of impressionistic technique or collage to convey his view of the city's complexity. It is not surprising to find allusions to Spanish ladies throughout. Lara was ever a lady's man. Generalissimo Franco appreciated Lara and in 1965 gave him a house in Granada. The Spanish erected a statue to Lara in Madrid.

Note the stellar job done by the trumpets in the accompaniment (e.g. in lines **8** and **10**). Such flair! They suggest the grandeur of what the city once was; the musical embellishments–appoggiaturas, etc. — are in harmony with the ornate complexity of Moorish architecture. Musical instruments add their own special color to enhance the beauty of a song.

Language Points

- line **2**: *Cantar* here is a noun meaning "song".

- lines **7-8**: In addition to bullfights *ensangrentada* (steeped in blood) brings to mind certain blood-stained events in Spanish history, e.g. the invasion of Napoleon (the horrors of which Goya depicted with such power) and the appalling carnage of the Spanish Civil War (1936-39). Certain words in songs (as in poetry) are rich in associations and allusions of this kind.

- lines **9-10**: Going from Spanish idiom to English idiom these two lines would be: "A woman who still has the witchcraft of Moorish eyes."

- line **13**: *suave*. The meaning is *agradable a los sentidos:* agreeable to the senses.

- line **16-17**: *Manola cantada in coplas preciosas*: This is apparently an allusion to the late nineteenth century and the working class women of Madrid who dressed in a flamboyant zarzuela-type costume and had plenty of haughty insolence.

- line **19-21**: It is the custom to put flowers around the frames of paintings of the Madonna found in churches. The Virgin "Morena" probably alludes to the Virgin of Guadalupe, patron saint of Mexico.

Version in English

1. Granada, I'm falling under your spell,

2. And if you could speak, what a fascinating tale you would tell.

3. Of an age the world has long forgotten.

4. Of an age that weaves a silent magic in Granada today.

5. The dawn in the sky greets the day with a sigh for Granada,

6. For she can remember the splendor that once was Granada.

7. It still can be found in the hills all around as I wander along.

8. Entranced by the beauty before me,

9. Entranced by a land full of sunshine and flowers and song.

10. And when day is done and the sun starts to set in Granada,

11. I envy the blush of the snow-clad Sierra Nevada.

12. For soon it will welcome the stars while a thousand guitars,

13. Play a soft habanera.

14. Then moonlit Granada will live again: the glory of yesterday,

15. Romantic and gay.

A few of the lines (e.g. **5, 10**) are trite, in my opinion, but overall this is an imaginative rendering of the song in English and manages to capture much of the spirit of the original Spanish.

18.
La paloma

Sebastián de Iradier y Salaverri, Spain, 1863

Artist: Nana Mouskouri

Nana Mouskouri

FIRST VERSE

1. Cuando salí de la Habana
When I left Havana

2. ¡Válgame Dios!
God help me!

3. Nadie me ha visto salir
No one saw me leave

4. si no fui yo
if not myself.

5. y una linda guachinanga
And a pretty guachinanga.

6. como una flor
like a flower

7. se vino detrás de mí.
who came after me.

8. ¡Que sí, señor!
Oh yes, mister!

CHORUS

9. Si a tu ventana
If to your window

10. llega una paloma,
a dove arrives,

11. trátala con cariño
treat it with affection

12. que es mi persona.
because it is me.

13. Cuéntale tus amores,
Tell it (about) your loves,

14. bien de mi vida,
Goodness of my life,

15. Corónala de flores.
Crown her with flowers.

16. que es cosa mía.
because she is mine.

17. ¡Ay! ¡Chinita que sí!
Oh, my little dove, yes!

18. ¡Ay! ¡Que dame tu amor!
Oh, give me your love!

19. ¡Ay! ¡Que vente conmigo,
Oh, come with me,

20. chinita, a dónde vivo yo!
Chinita, to where I live!

Repeat 5-20, then 17-20.

General Notes

This song goes on for several more verses but I am including only the part that most singers sing. The parts that I have not included tell of their marriage in the cathedral and some speculation on the number of children they will have: at least seven and as many as fifteen "guachinanguitos." The composer of this song, Sebastián Iradier, was born in Spain in 1809 and visited Cuba in 1861. It was there that he got the idea for *La paloma*, which appeared in 1863. The story of doves being able to carry souls possibly originates with the sinking of the Persian fleet in a storm in 492 B. C.

This song (with the charming 1938 version of the 'Chilean nightingale', Rosita Serrano) appears in the movie *Das Boot* (1981) in which even hardened German submariners respond to its delicate charm. *La paloma* is also nicely woven into the fabric of the movie *Juárez* where it is presented as the favorite song of the Empress Carlota, wife of the ill-fated Maximilian. (See photo.) Maximilian is shot by a firing squad in Mexico; Carlota ends up in a mental institution in France.

The Empress Carlota

Iradier's habanera, "El Arreglito" (1864) is remarkably like Bizet's "Habanera" in the opera "Carmen" (1875). When pressed, Bizet admitted it but said he had thought the song was in the popular tradition and therefore without copyright problems. Try Youtubing "Habanera and Maria Callas" for a real treat.

There are other good artists to check out on YouTube e.g. Rosita Serrano, Victoria de los Ángeles and Dean Martin.

Sebastián de Iradier y Salaverri,
composer of "La paloma"

Language Points

- line **5**: *guachinanga*. This word usually means a red snapper but here it is a term of endearment for a woman. Go figure!

- line **17**: *Chinita*: I couldn't find good explanations of either of these words. *Chinita* can sometimes mean something along the lines of "my girl". See my earlier remarks in the section "Endearments in Spanish" (p.24).

- lines **17-19**: *Ay!* eludes translation and can have many meanings.

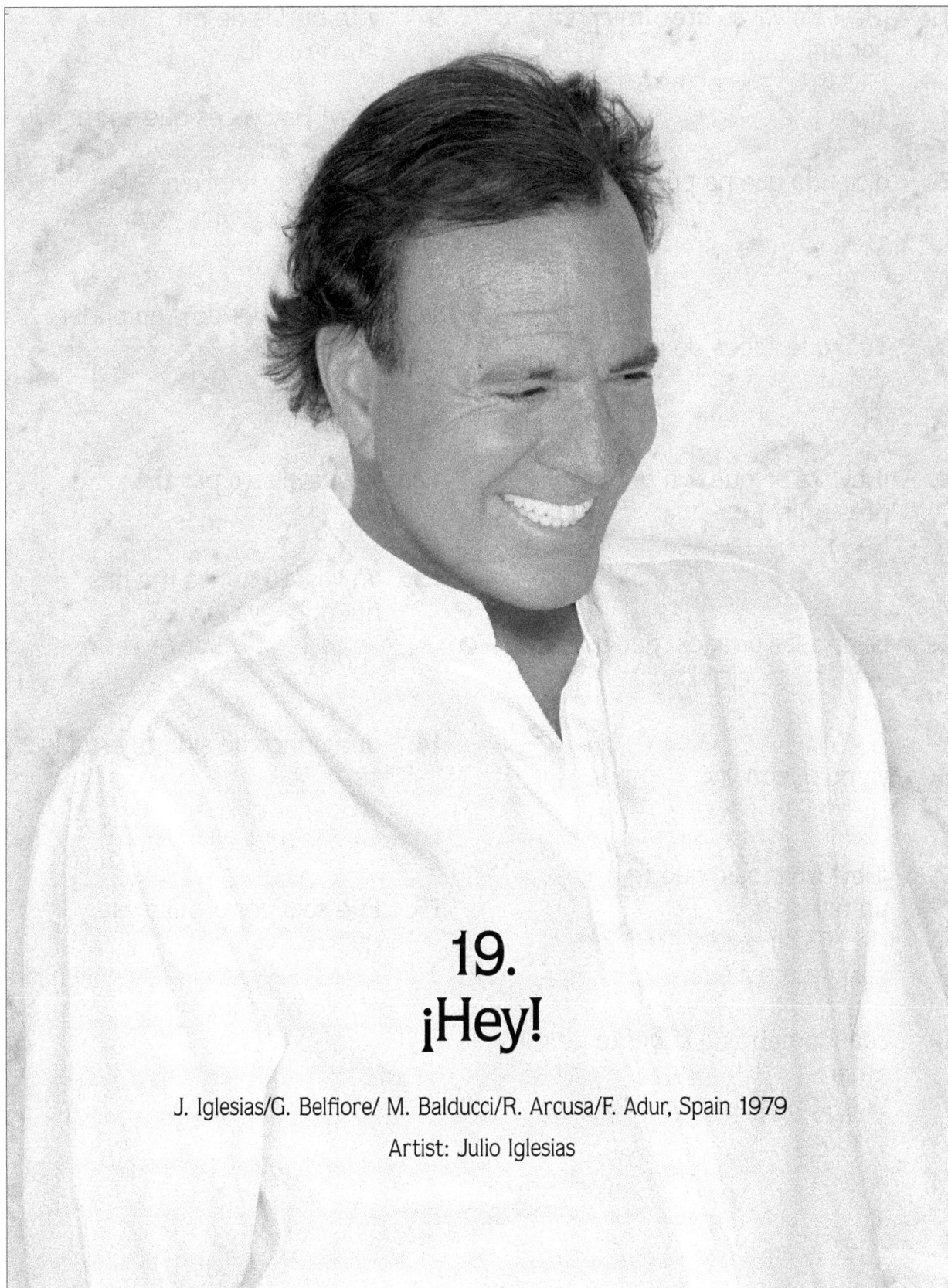

19.
¡Hey!

J. Iglesias/G. Belfiore/ M. Balducci/R. Arcusa/F. Adur, Spain 1979

Artist: Julio Iglesias

1. **¡Hey! No vayas presumiendo por ahí**
Hey! Don't go putting on airs around here

2. **diciendo que no puedo estar sin ti,**
Saying that I can't 'exist' without you.

3. **Tú, ¿qué sabes de mí?**
You, what do you know about me?

4. **¡Hey! Ya sé que a ti te gusta presumir,**
Hey! I know that you like to put on airs

5. **decir a los amigos que sin ti**
(And) say to friends that without you

6. **ya no puedo vivir.**
I (really) can't live.

7. **¡Hey! No creas que te haces un favor**
Hey ! Don't believe that you're doing yourself a favor

8. **cuando hablas a la gente de mi amor**
When you speak to people of my love

9. **y te burlas de mí.**
And make fun of me.

10. **¡Hey! Hay veces que es mejor querer así**
Hey! There are times when it is better to love this way (i.e. my way)

11. **que ser querido y no poder sentir**
Than (it is) to be loved and not be able to feel

12. **lo que siento por ti.**
What I feel for you.

13. **Ya ves, tú nunca me has querido, ¿ya lo ves?**
You see, you have never loved me, do you see it now?

14. **que nunca he sido tuyo ya lo sé.**
That I never have been yours, I know that now.

15. **Fue solo por orgullo ese querer.**
It was only out of pride, that (kind of)love of yours.

16. Ya ves de qué te vale ahora presumir
Now you really see what pride gets you

17. ahora que no estoy ya junto a ti
Now that I am not beside you

18. ¿Qué les dirás de mí?
What will you tell them about me?

19. ¡Hey! recuerdo que ganabas siempre tú,
Hey! I remember that you always won,

20. que hacías de ese triunfo una virtud.
That you made of that triumph a virtue.

21. Yo era sombra y tú luz.
I was shadow and you were light.

22. ¡Hey! No sé si tú también recordarás
Hey! I don't know if you too will recall

23. que siempre yo intentaba hacer la paz.
That I was the one who always tried to make peace.

24. Yo era un río en tu mar.
I was a river in your sea.

25 Repeat verses 13-18.

26. ¡Hey! Ahora que ya todo terminó,
Hey! Now that everything has ended

27. que como siempre soy el perdedor
And that, as always, I am the loser

28. cuando pienses en mí.
When you think of me.

29. ¡Hey! No creas que te guardo algún rencor
Hey! Don't believe that I harbor any rancor.

30. Es siempre más feliz quien más amó
Whoever loved most is the happiest.

31. y ése siempre fui yo.
And I was always that (person).

Repeat: 13-15 twice.

General Notes

Julio Iglesias made this song famous. Watch him sing it on YouTube. I can recall wandering through the streets of Gerona in Spain one balmy June evening in 1988 and hearing Julio sing this song through outdoor speakers which had been placed on street corners throughout the city. What a magnificent tribute for a singer! And how powerful a role music and language play in helping people to form a cohesive sense of national identity!

This gem of a song from 1979 develops the theme of loving someone who doesn't return your love and who seems to continue in the relationship for merely selfish reasons: to glory in her own power and even to boast to her friends how she has this poor sucker in tow. He thinks she is locked into her own little world of Narcissism and that she will be punished by her inability to ever feel true love for anyone. All very well, yet I get the impression that he is not really over it at all. He obsesses about her throughout the song and the tone of the music is a curious mixture of reproach and wistfulness. Maybe the poor guy has a problem with co-dependency.

The dictionary describes "hey" as follows: "an exclamation used to get one's attention." "Hey" as a title seems to me trite and vague and I would imagine that it has done very little to generate interest in this beautiful song. A good title can make all the difference.

- line **13**: The trumpets here add drama and drive the melody along with their 'shot notes'.

The oboe is used effectively to suggest isolation and sadness (lines **17, 19-22**).

If you like *¡Hey!* I would recommend another song with similar merits: Charles Aznavour's "Hier Encore" (the English version is called *Yesterday when I was young*). "Hier Encore" and *¡Hey!* are unusual in that they discuss love (and the inability to love) at considerable length. *¡Hey!* probes vanity, narcissism and callousness. The narrator of Aznavour's song confesses to the sins of his youth-- his own arrogance and insensitivity towards the women in his life. In both these songs their very length becomes a virtue. See my Appendix on p. 119 for further details.

Language Points

The narrator's main reproach is her need to show off and be the center of attention. This is conveyed by the verb *presumir* (lines **1, 4, 16** and **32**). *Presumir* is a word used to convey pride and pretentiousness and putting on airs. The English word "presume" is a deceptive cognate and has a different meaning.

I find an advanced Spanish dictionary (e.g., *El Diccionario didactico avanzado*, Ediciones SM) useful for its exact definitions. Here is how my dictionary defines *presumir*: *Referido a una persona, cuidar mucho su aspecto externo para aparecer atractiva* (Referring to a person, to take great care with one's external appearance in order to appear attractive.) Studying with a "Spanish only" dictionary helps you to think in Spanish and is an interesting activity in itself.

- line **9**: *te burlas,* from *burlarse,* to make fun of, mock. A proud person would be prone to mockery ("burlar"). Some people, for example Voltaire and Fernando Díaz-Plaja have seen pride as Spain's national flaw. Who knows?

- line **15**: *ese querer,* i.e. her kind of love, leading him on without really caring about him, boasting to her friends about her power over him. *Querer* is a verb which is used as a noun.

- line **17**: *junto a ti* resists accurate translation. The best I can suggest is "close to you".

- line **20**: *Que hacías de ese triunfo una virtud.* That you made of this triumph a virtue (that you made a virtue of this triumph)

Thus does this somewhat perverse narcissist rationalize: "Oh, maybe I win all the time (line **19**) but it has nothing to do with any deficiencies in me, it only shows that I am superior and always in the right." A brilliant verse.

- line **21**: *Yo era sombra y tu luz.* A simple metaphor and it is pure poetry, likening their love to powerful forces in nature. The same can be said of line **24**, *Era río en tu mar.*

Being Spanish, Julio Iglesias naturally pronounces words with a Castilian accent. In Castilian intervocalic "c" and "z" are pronounced "th". This comes through in *decir* (line **5**), *haces* (line **7**), *veces* (line **10**), *hacías* (line **20**); *luz* (line **21**), *paz* (line **23**), and *feliz* (line **30**).

The opening words to *¡Hey!* in English:

"Hey! It's wonderful to see you once again!
To see your smile and hear you call my name...."

This English adaptation totally lacks the complex irony and subtlety of the original.

Notes

20.
Mi Buenos Aires querido

Gardel & Le Pera, Argentina, 1934

Artist: Carlos Gardel

Buenos Aires

INTRODUCTION

1. **Mi Buenos Aires querido**
My Buenos Aires beloved

2. **cuándo yo te vuelva a ver**
When I see you again

3. **no habrá más penas ni olvido.**
There will no longer be sorrow(s) or forgetting.

FIRST VERSE

4. **El farolito de la calle en que nací**
The little street lamp in the street where I was born

5. **fue el centinela de mis promesas de amor.**
Was the sentinel for my promises of love.

6. **Bajo su inquieta lucecita yo la vi**
Under its restless (i.e. flickering) light I saw her,

7. **a mi pebeta luminosa como un sol.**
My little babe, luminous as a sun.

8. **Hoy que la suerte quiere que te vuelva a ver,**
Today, now that fortune wants me to see you again,

9. **ciudad porteña de mi único querer,**
Port city of my one and only love,

10. **oigo la queja de un bandoneón**
I hear the lament of a bandoneon

11. **dentro de mi pecho pide rienda el corazón.**
In my breast my heart asks for some slack.

12. **Mi Buenos Aires, tierra florida**
My Buenos Aires, flowery land

13. **dónde mi vida terminaré.**
Where I will end my days.

14. **Bajo tu amparo no hay desengaño.**
Under your shelter there is no disappointment.

15. **Vuelan los años, se olvida el dolor.**
The years fly by, pain is forgotten.

16. **En caravana los recuerdos pasan**
In caravan formation memories pass by

17. **como una estela dulce de emoción.**
Like a sweet trail of emotion.

18. Quiero que sepas que al evocarte
I want you (Buenos Aires) to know that when I evoke you

19. se van las penas del corazón.
The aches of the heart go away.

SECOND VERSE

20. Las ventanitas de mis calles de Arrabal
The little windows of my streets of Arrabal

21. dónde sonríe una muchachita en flor,
Where a little girl in the flower of youth (paraphrase) smiles,

22. quiero de nuevo yo volver a contemplar
I want to gaze at once again

23. aquellos ojos que acarician al mirar.
Those eyes that caress you when they look at you.

24. En la cortada más maleva una canción
In the roughest alley a song

25. dice su ruego de coraje y de pasión.
Says its prayer for courage and passion;

26. Una promesa y un suspirar,
(It is both) a promise and a sigh,

27. borró una lágrima de pena aquel cantar.
Wiped away a tear of sorrow that singing.

[26-27: That singing, which is both a promise and a sigh, wiped away a tear of sorrow.]

Repeat 1-3.

General Notes

In *Mi Buenos Aires querido* the narrator reminisces tenderly on the city (particularly the barrio of Arrabal), the young ladies whom he pursued in his youth, and the pleasures of dancing the tango to the accompaniment of a bandoneon. The theme of nostalgia dominates the song. If you visit the Museo dell'emigrazione (formerly in Rome's Vittorio Emmanuele monument but recently relocated to Genoa) you will see many vintage photos (ca 1870-1914) of Italians who are about to leave their beautiful, poverty-stricken land. Thousands of them are bound for Buenos Aires. Their faces are haunting in their grim sadness; do they know at some obscure level that they will forever keep Italy close to their hearts? They will, and the bitter-sweetness of nostalgia will torment many of them for the rest of their lives. When the tango composers among them or their offspring come to write tangos in Buenos Aires it is almost inevitable that nostalgia will be one of the dominant themes: it is a theme which they have known well for a long time and is probably hard-wired to them like a family script.

On the day I visited the Museum they were playing music on the loudspeakers. One of the songs was *Addio a Napoli*, as sung by Enrico Caruso, himself a Neapolitan. It was a brilliant choice of background music because this song conveys so well the heart-wrenching feelings of being forced to leave one's country.

Enrico Caruso

See my Appendix at the end of this book and you can read the original Italian words and the English translation.

Around six million people emigrated to Argentina between 1880 and 1930. About 50 per cent of these people were Italian and many of these were from Genoa.

According to Asher Benatar in his eloquent and beautifully illustrated book, *Tango* (Buenos Aires, Ars editors, 1992) in its formative stages tango was influenced by the typical melodies of the Cuban habanera and the strong beat of the candombe, an African dance.

short in an airplane crash in the area of Medellín, Colombia in 1935. Also killed in the crash was his collaborator, lyricist Alfredo Le Pera. There is a Carlos Gardel Museum in the Abasto district of Buenos Aires and a movie about his life, *La vida de Carlos Gardel* (1939).

Google the following url for a charming scene in the movie *Mi Buenos Aires querido* where Gardel stands on the deck of a ship looking out at Buenos Aires and breaks into song. Beside him stands the captain who listens to him attentively and clearly shares his emotion. Probably most Porteños would feel the same way. See https://www.youtube.com/watch?v=m3ickPixoal for the clip.

Carlos Gardel

There is much debate about many aspects of Carlos Gardel's life. He was born in Toulouse (of uncertain paternal parentage) in 1890 but moved to Buenos Aires with his mother at age three. His career was many-sided: writer of tango music, singer and movie actor. He wrote several famous tangos, including *Por una cabeza* (which is the tango Al Pacino dances to in the 1992 movie *Scent of a Woman.*) During the 1920s and 1930s Gardel was proably the main force behind the increasingly widespread popularity of the Argentine tango. Perhaps his two most famous movies are *El día que me quieras* and *Mi Buenos Aires querido* (1936 and a remake in 1962). Gardel's life was cut

Language Points

- line **2**: *Vuelva* followed by *a ver* conveys the idea of "again", e.g. *volvió a llover:* it rained again.

- lines **4-6**: The composer attributes emotion to an object (*el farolito*), another example of the pathetic fallacy mentioned in my notes on *Caminito* (song 11).

- line **5**: *centinela.* Like a sentinel (one thinks of Leporello in "Don Giovanni") the street lamp stands guard for him, ready to tip him off if any danger, e.g. a rival, presents itself during his night-time excursions in pursuit of romance.

- line **6:** *inquieta*: worried, troubled. It suggests flickering (of the street light) but it also suggests that it is the narrator himself who experiences these restless feelings. Another possible meaning is *"interesado por descubrir cosas nuevas"* (interested in discovering new things). *Diccionario Didáctico.*

- line **7:** *pebeta* is Lunfardo for a young woman. It would translate as "Babe", "Honey-bun", etc. Lunfardo was originally the slang used by criminals in Buenos Aires. Over the years its usage spread and some of it surfaced in tango bars, tango dance halls, etc.

- line **9:** *Porteño* refers to a person from Buenos Aires. *Mi único querer* can refer to the girl (his one and only love) or to the city itself (his beloved home town).

- line **11:** *Dentro de mi pecho pide rienda el corazón* This literally means *asks for the reins.* The sense seems to be that his heart asks for some slack so that he can maybe drop the macho reserve and give freer rein to his emotion.

- lines **16-17:** The sense of these two lines is "In caravan formation memories pass by, leaving sweet emotions in their wake."

- line **20:** *calles de Arrabal*: Arrabal is one of the poor barrios of Buenos Aires in which the tango took root and flourished.

- line **24:** *maleva* in tango lyrics means rough, dangerous, crime-infested.

- line **26-27:** In more prosaic syntax: That singing, which is a promise and a sigh, wiped away a tear of sorrow.

Spanish makes frequent use of affectionate diminutive endings (suffixes) and in this song they convey the tenderness which the narrator feels: farolito (4), lucecita (6), ventanitas (20), muchachita (21).

21.
El día que me quieras

Gardel and Le Pera, Argentina, 1935
Artist: Carlos Gardel

INTRODUCTION

1. Acaricia mi ensueño
Caresses my reverie

2. el suave murmullo
the smooth murmur

3. de tu suspirar.
of your sighs.
[The smooth murmur of your sighs caresses my reverie.]

4. Cómo ríe la vida
How life laughs

5. si tus ojos negros
if your dark eyes

6. me quieren mirar,
want to gaze at me

7. y si es mío el amparo
And if it is mine, the shelter

8. de tu risa leve
of your light laughter

9. que es como un cantar.
which is like singing.

10. Ella aquieta mi herida;
It salves my wound;

11. todo, todo se olvida.
everything is forgotten.

VERSE ONE

12. El día que me quieras
The day that you love me

13. la rosa que engalana
the rose which adorns (i. e. the beauty-giving rose)

14. se vestirá de fiesta
will clothe itself in festive garb

15. con su mejor color,
with its best color

16. y al viento las campanas
and to the wind the church bells

17. dirán que ya eres mía,
will say that you are mine

(16-17: And the church bells will say to the wind that you are mine.)

18. y locas las fontanas
and the fountains, gone crazy,

19. se cantarán tu amor.
will sing to each other (of) your love.

VERSE TWO

20. La noche que me quieras
The night that you love me

21. desde el azul del cielo
from the blue of the sky

22. las estrellas celosas
the stars, jealous,

23. nos mirarán pasar.
will watch us pass by.

24. Y un rayo misterioso
And a mysterious ray

25. hará nido en tu pelo,
Will make its nest in your hair,

26. luciérnaga curiosa
A curious glowworm

27. que verá que eres
which will see that you are

28. mi consuelo.
My delight.

[In Carlos Gardel's version lines 29
to 41 are spoken, not sung.]

VERSE THREE

29. El día que me quieras
The day that you love me

30. no habrá más que armonía.
there will be only harmony.

31. Será clara la aurora
The dawn will be bright

32. y alegre el manantial.
and the spring will be happy.

33. Traerá quieta la brisa
The breeze, quieted down, will bring

34. rumor de melodía.
the sound of a melody.

35. Y nos darán las fuentes
And will give to us the fountains

36. su canto de cristal.
Their crystal sound.

35-36: And the fountains will give
to us their crystal sound.

VERSE FOUR

37. El día que me quieras
The day that you love me

38. endulzará sus cuerdas
will sweeten his chords

39. el pájaro cantor.
the song bird.

40. Florecerá la vida.
Life will burst into flower.

41. No existirá el dolor.
Sorrow will not exist.

[Lines 42 to 50 are sung.]

VERSE FIVE`

42. La noche que me quieras,
The night that you love me

43. desde el azul del cielo
from the blue of the sky

44. las estrellas celosas
the jealous stars

45. nos mirarán pasar.
will watch us pass by.

46. Y un rayo misterioso
And a mysterious ray

47. hará nido en tu pelo,
will make its nest in your hair,

48. luciérnaga curiosa
a curious glowworm

49. que verá que eres
which will see that you are

50. mi consuelo.
my delight.

General Notes

- Line **11**: An introduction like this adds much to a song by creating atmosphere. Songs like *Noche de ronda* (3) and *Granada* (17) are also effective in this way.

Language Points

This is a difficult song to translate because it is couched in ethereal language and the poetic images work much better in Spanish than they do in English.

- line **14**: This is more paraphrase than translation.

- line **16-19**: I mentioned how the pathetic fallacy is used in *Caminito* (song 11). It is used even more extensively here. If and when this lady decides to return his love all of nature will collude: roses will be extraordinarily beautiful (verses 13-15), church bells will proclaim their love (16-17), the stars will become jealous (21-23), etc.

- line **28** and **50**: *Consuelo* — *Alívio de la pena o del dolor que afligen y oprimen el ánimo* i.e. relief from the suffering and grief which afflict and weigh heavily on the spirit (*Diccionario didáctico avanzado, Ediciones S.M.*).

- line **32**: *manantial* means spring in the sense of clear water gurgling out of the rocks.

- line: **37-39**: The day that you love me the songbird will sweeten his chords.

- line **41**: *dolor* in tango lyrics means sorrow rather than pain.

Throughout the song the singer drops the final "s": *campanas* (line **16**); *quieras* (line **20, 29, 42**). This tendency is typical of *porteño* Spanish.

Notes

22.
A media luz

E. Donato, music & C. Lenzi, words, Argentina, 1924
Artist: Julio Iglesias

Photo of Al Pacino in "Scent of a Woman"

1. Corrientes tres- cuatro- ocho
Corrientes Street, three, four, eight

2. segundo piso, ascensor.
Second floor, elevator.

3. No hay porteros, ni vecinos,
There are no doormen nor
neighbors

4. adentro coctel y amor.
Inside (there is) a cocktail and
love.

5. Pisito que puso Maple,
A small floor space installed by
Maple's furniture store,

6. piano, estera y velador,
(a) piano, a straw rug and a night
table,

7. un telefón que contesta,
a telephone which answers

8. una vitrola que llora
a gramophone which sobs

9. viejos tangos de mi flor
old tangos wonderful

10. y un gato de porcelana
and a porcelain cat

11. pa'que no maulle al amor.
so that it won't meow at love

CHORUS

12. Y todo a media luz,
And everything (is) in half-light,

13. a media luz los dos
In half-light the two of us

14. a media luz los besos
in half-light kisses

15. a media luz los dos.
in half-light the two of us.

16. Y todo a media luz,
and everything in half-light

17. ¡Qué brujo es el amor!
How bewitching love is!

18. A media luz los besos
In half-light, kisses,

19. a media luz los dos.
In half-light, the two of us.

Repeat 1-19 then 12-19

Robert Stuart Thomson

General Notes

This version of *A media luz* contains an introduction featuring that classic instrument of the Argentinian tango, the bandoneón.

The terse style of this song–short quick impressions conveyed by phrases–is well suited to the somewhat staccato music of the tango. Just random memories, but taken together they convey the atmosphere of a secret rendezvous. The visitor's senses have been quickened by the anticipated pleasures awaiting and thus attuned it seems that they will be able to recall the strangest little details. The impressionistic technique recalls Lara's *Granada* (song 17). It also recalls, for me anyway, that haunting American classic of 1936, *These Foolish Things*:

A cigarette that bears a lipstick's traces.

An airline ticket to romantic places.

And still my heart has wings.

These foolish things

Remind me of you.

A tinkling piano in the next apartment.

Those stumbling words that told you

What my heart meant.

A fairground's painted swings.

These foolish things

Remind me of you.

For a treat, google "These Foolish Things" and Ella Fitzgerald or Frank Sinatra.

Language Points

- line **1**: at its height in the 1940s Corrientes Street (in Buenos Aires) was the location of a number of famous tango haunts: Tango Bar, Café Nacional, the Marzotto, etc.

- line **5**: Maple is a high quality furniture store in Buenos Aires.

- line **9**: *de mi flor* means something like wonderful.

- line **17**: *brujo* (wizard) is used a lot in Spanish cultures to convey the mystery of love and perhaps its fatal power. A famous Spanish movie, *El amor brujo*, is just one example of many.

On the subject of movies, I would recommend *Tango Bar* (1987) which shows how the Argentine tango evolved over the years and radically altered its form in some countries, e.g. the U.S.A. and Great Britain. *Scent of a Woman* (1992) stars Al Pacino in the role of a blind retired U.S. Army officer who surprises everyone by dancing the tango "Por una cabeza" in an upscale New York bar. In *Assassination Tango* (2002) Robert Duvall plays a hit-man sent to Buenos Aires to kill one of the generals implicated in the *Dirty War (La Guerra Sucia)* of the 1970s.

The constant repetition of *A media luz* conveys the obsessiveness of lust and the inexplicable tenacity of certain memories in life.

Notes

23.
Que nadie sepa mi sufrir

Ángel Cabral (music) and Enrique Dizeo (words). Argentina, 1936
Artist: Plácido Domingo

Plácido Domingo

1. **No te asombres si te digo lo que fuiste:**
   Don't be amazed if I tell you what you were:

2. **una ingrata con mi pobre corazón,**
   an ungrateful person with my poor heart

3. **porque el fuego de tus lindos ojos negros**
   because the fire of your beautiful dark eyes

4. **alumbraron el camino de otro amor.**
   illuminated the pathway of another love.

5. **Y pensar que te adoraba tiernamente,**
   And to think that I adored you tenderly,

6. **que a tu lado como nunca me sentí.**
   and that I felt better than ever by your side.

7. **¡Ay! amor de mis amores, reina mia,**
   Oh, love of my loves, my queen,

8. **¿Qué me hiciste que no puedo conformarme**
   What have you done to me so that I can't be satisfied

9. **sin poderte contemplar?**
   unless I can gaze at you.

10. **Ya que pagaste mal a mi cariño tan sincero,**
    Since you repaid badly my affection so sincere

11. **lo que conseguirás que no te nombre nunca más.**
    What you will get from this is that I will never mention your name ever again.

12. **Amor de mis amores, si dejaste de quererme,**
    Love of my loves, if you have stopped loving me

13. **no hay cuidado que la gente de eso no se enterará.**
    There's no danger that people will find out about that.

14. **¿Qué gano con decir que una mujer cambió mi suerte?**
    What do I gain by saying that a woman changed my fortune?

15. **Se burlarán de mí; que nadie sepa mi sufrir.**
    They will make fun of me; let no one know of my suffering.

Robert Stuart Thomson

General Notes

The narrator is concerned about his reputation (maybe his honor as well) and the gossip that might be circulating. The worst that can happen is that he will appear to be ridiculous. This seems to be more of a concern in Latin countries than in English-speaking countries. We have seen it already in *Di que no es verdad* (song 15, line 3) and in *¡Hey!* (song 19).

In 1957 *Que nadie sepa mi sufrir* was taken up in France by Edith Piaf who radically changed the words and title, renaming it *La Foule.*

Language Points

• line 4: *alumbraron:* Contrastive darkness and light are used in several songs e.g. *¡Ay! ¡Qué vida tan oscura!* (song 9). In the tropics the sun is dazzling and the nights very dark. It figures that these phenomena would be reflected in the imagery of songs, poetry, etc.

Notes

24.
Las mañanitas

Origin Unknown

Basilica of Our Lady of Guadalupe in Mexico City. Every year on the night of December eleventh mañanitas are sung here to honor Nuestra Señora de Guadalupe

VERSE ONE

1 Qué linda está la mañana en que vengo a saludarte.
How beautiful is the morning on which I come to greet you.

2 Venimos todos reunidos con gusto a felicitarte.
We all come together with pleasure to congratulate you.

3 El día que tú naciste nacieron todas las flores.
The day that you were born all the flowers sprouted.

4 En la pila del bautizo cantaron los ruiseñores.
In the baptismal font the nightingales sang.

5 Ya viene amaneciendo, ya la luz del día nos dio.
It is already dawning, already the light of day to us it has given.

6 Levántate de mañana, mira que ya amaneció.
Rise up early, look and see that it's already dawned.

VERSE TWO

7 Quisiera ser solecito para entrar por tu ventana
I would like to be a little sun to come through your window

8 y darte los buenos días acostadita en la cama.
And give (wish) you a good day as you lie nice and snug in bed.

9 Quisiera ser un San Juan, quisiera ser un San Pedro
I would like to be a Saint John, I would like to be a Saint Peter

10 para venirte a saludar con la música del cielo.
To be able to come and greet you with the music of heaven.

12 Con jazmines y flores hoy te vengo a saludar.
With jasmines and (other) flowers today I come to greet you.

13 Hoy por ser día de tu santo te venimos a cantar.
Today because it is the day of your saint we come to sing to you.

General Notes

There are many other verses to this charming song which is traditionally played on the morning of someone's birthday or saint's day.

It is not found in our version of *Las mañanitas* but many other versions start with two beautiful lines: "Estas son las mañanitas/ que cantaba el rey David." Google the title and try another version of the song.

Try googling *Las mañanitas* and in the Wikipedia entry you will find several articles and a couple of books. The resources of the Internet seem endless.

Language Points

- line **5**: To put this in more natural English: "It is already dawning and already it (the dawn) has given us the light of day."

- line **8**: *acostadita* eludes translation so I have used a paraphrase to get close to the feelings inherent in this word.

Notes

Suggestions to Teachers

How to Present Songs

Teaching a language with songs is a dynamic, memorable way to enhance your program (which I assume includes grammar explanations, drills, readings, conversation, etc.) As students work with songs they develop oral understanding, good punctuation and 'rhythm' i.e. sensitivity to the distinctive musicality of Spanish, and insight into the culture of the country which gave birth to the song. I have used songs a lot in my teaching and find them invaluable.

There are two methods that you can use:

(a) *The integral text method* i.e. you give to the students all the words to a song. There are no blanks to fill in. Use this method if you are teaching a course on songs.

(b *The cloze method* in which you elicit from your students the words that you have omitted in the cloze outline that they work from. This is the best method for teaching a specific language point (a verb tense, a grammar point, or an idiom). Below are the details for teaching both methods.

A. The Integral Text Method (Outline)

1 Choose a song and find the words to it.

2 Type up song in Spanish. Triple space, number the lines.

3 Photocopy enough copies for class.

4 Find a recording of the song to use in class.

5 Set up classroom with screen or whiteboard, CD player, etc.

6 Class begins: Explain point of exercise.

7 Give each student a copy of the words in Spanish.

8 Explain background (singer, etc.) Play song, pointing to words.

9 Students print their translation of nouns and verbs as you play a second time.

10 Go over their answers to nouns and verbs section.

11 Students print translation of adjectives and adverbs as you play a third time.

12 Go over their answers to the adjectives and adverbs exercise.

13 Students figure out remaining words as you play a fourth time.

14 Go over answers to remaining words.

15 Have students apply criteria as they listen to song a fifth time.

16 Discuss the merits of the song.

The Integral Text Method (Details)

In this method you use a complete version of the song, not clozes. The instructions below might contain more information than you need so amend them to suit your own needs.

Before using songs in the classroom I suggest rereading two sections: *How to approach each song* (located just before song 2) and *What to appreciate in the songs* (located just before song 3).

Steps to follow:

1 Choose a song and find the words to it. It is best to select a song which is beautiful in its own right and which can be used to teach specific things: a grammar point, an idiom, a verb tense, a cultural aspect, etc. *Cucurrucucú, paloma* (song 8) provides a good exercise on the imperfect tense. *Piel canela* (song 13) provides an excellent overview of the subjunctive. And so on. The Internet is useful for finding the words to a song. I usually google YouTube and then enter search words, something like "*Solamente una vez*, letras" (or "*Solamente una vez* and words" or "*Solamente una vez* and lyrics." Internet versions often contain errors so you might have to look at more than one. If you use any of the songs in this book you will find the Spanish and English versions reliable.

2 When typing up your Spanish words to the song follow the format that I have used throughout this book and make sure that there is plenty of space between each line. Your students will need space to write in an accurate word for word translation. Be sure to number each line (1, 2, 3, etc.). This will make for easy reference once you start teaching the song.

3 Photocopy enough copies for your class and print a few extra copies in case you need them.

4 Get a recording of the song (CD, YouTube, mp3, or even DVD). I use a CD of Vicente Fernández for song six, *Angelitos negros*. I play this song at least three times then I conclude the lesson by showing a clip from a DVD of the movie, *Angelitos negros* starring Pedro Infante.

5 Set up the classroom so that you can project the words to the song on a screen or white board (or even a bare wall). I use an overhead projector and screen. If you use an overhead projector you will have to get acetate sheets on which to print, not write, the words to the song. I prepare my own acetates using a dark felt pen with permanent ink (This will avoid smudging in case you want to use them again.) I print the words clearly in upper case letters and it works just fine. Power Point might work but I don't see how you could print the English translation as it unfolds, which is such an interesting, dynamic part of the process. If you prefer to use neither overhead projector nor Power Point print the words on the blackboard or on a large whiteboard.

6 If necessary, explain to your class the value of the exercise (I outlined these in the sections *"How to approach each song"* and *"What to look for in songs"*.) Students need to know that working on songs hones listening skills and pronunciation and develops vocabulary. It also helps them to learn grammar rules, verb tenses, and idioms not to mention opening their eyes to cultural differences. A beautiful song also is worth studying as poetry in its own right. The ideal is to memorize a song. That way it will be with them all their life.

7 Give each student a copy of the Spanish words to the song. (You will have printed up enough copies for everyone in the class.) Explain that their final goal is to end up with a good accurate translation.

8 You are all set to go. This is a good time to tell your students the background of the song: when it was composed, who wrote it, which recording artist they will hear. Mention any interesting background (e.g., Nat King Cole's trip to Latin America if you are listening to *¿Quizás? ¿quizás? ¿quizás?*). Now *play the song*. As the song plays, point on the acetate (or the blackboard or whatever)

to where the singer is. This helps the students to follow, phrase by phrase. I emphasize phrases because the students' eventual goal is to be able to speak Spanish with all its distinctive musicality. This is often a good time to comment on Spanish phonetics.

9 Play the song *a second time* but before starting ask students to look for nouns and verbs (and possibly subjects and predicates) and print the English equivalents directly below the Spanish words. When the song is over go through it line by line, eliciting from your students where the nouns and verbs are and what they mean. Identifying subjects, predicates, etc. is optional and will depend on your clientele. As you elicit the words, print them on the acetate sheet or screen. Use an erasable felt pen because you might want to erase the English words and use the acetate again. This is a good group exercise and there is no need to rush it. It should be done carefully. Students monitor their own work.

10 You are now ready to play the song *for the third time*. Ask the students to look for adjectives, adverbs, exclamations, etc. After you have played the song elicit from your students a translation of the adjectives, adverbs, etc. As usual, have them print the English words directly below their Spanish equivalents.

11 Go over the song *a fourth time*. This time students translate all the remaining words. When they have heard the whole song, go over the correct answers. This is the time to explain idioms, etc. This is a good exercise for showing that grammar and a knowledge of vocabulary do not explain idioms and that translation is a complex affair.

12 Play the song *for the fifth time* then ask your students what they think of it. What are the merits (or even shortcomings) of the song, in their opinion? Are there any culturally specific allusions? Any good metaphors, etc.? Review *"What to appreciate in the songs"* (just after song 2).

13 An option here is to play a recording of the song by a different artist and compare this version with the one they have been working on.

I have written at length on the "Integral text method." You might choose to amend some of the steps or even skip them entirely. Whatever works! The other way of teaching with songs is to use cloze outlines.

B. The Cloze Method (Outline)

1 Choose a song suitable for your teaching objective.

2 Type up song in Spanish: triple spaced, number the lines.

3 White out the words that you want students to find.

4 Photocopy enough copies for class.

5 Find a recording of the song to use in class.

6 Set up classroom with screen or whiteboard, CD player, etc.

7 Give each student a copy of the cloze.

8 Explain the point of the exercise, e.g. a review of verbs. The task is to fill in the blanks.

9 Play song, pointing to words as it plays.

10 Elicit correct answers from students; print them on screen or board. Students correct their own work.

11 Play song again if they did not find all the verbs.

12 Discuss merits of song and/or do a review of verbs.

The Cloze Method (Details)

In case you don't know, a cloze outline is a copy of the words to a song with key words whited out (or somehow deleted). Clozes work very well if you are not teaching a whole course on songs but only want to use a song to teach something specific such as verb tenses, a grammar point, an idiom, etc. They also work well as a review or just a pleasant activity which will add some spice to everyone's life.

Let's suppose that you want to teach (or review) verbs, past and present, with a good song. Rich in verbs, song 14 would be a good choice. Here are the steps:

• Find the complete words to the song. Type them on a page. Youtube is a good place to start but beware of errors. To fine-tune the lyrics listen to a few versions of the song on Youtube.

• Number the lines of the song (1, 2, 3, etc.). This will facilitate reference later when you discuss the song in class. Double-space or triple-space the lines so that the page doesn't look cluttered.

• Go through the song and delete all the verbs (There are 23 of them.)

• Print underline marks where the verbs were.

• This is your cloze outline. Print sufficient copies for your class plus a few extras in case some get ruined.

Compare the two versions below (the complete version followed by the cloze based on it) and you will see what I mean. Here is the complete version:

¿Y qué hiciste del amor que me juraste?

1. ¿Y qué hiciste del amor que me juraste?

2. ¿Y qué has hecho de los besos que te di?

3. ¿Y qué excusa puedes darme si faltaste

4. y mataste la esperanza que hubo en mí?

5. ¡Y qué ingrato es el destino que me hiere!

6. ¡Y qué absurda la razón de mi pasión!

7. ¡Y qué necio es este amor que no se muere

8. y prefiere perdonarte tu traición!

9. Y pensar que en mi vida fuiste flama

10. y el caudal de mi gloria fuiste tu

11. y llegué a quererte con el alma

12. y hoy me mata de tristeza tu actitud.

13. ¿Y a qué debo, dime, entonces, tu abandono?

14. ¿Y en qué ruta tu promesa se perdió?

15. Y si dices la verdad yo te perdono

16. y te llevo en mi recuerdo junto a Dios.

Repeat lines 9-16.

Here is how your cloze will look once you delete the words that you want your students to find (in this case it's the verbs) and leave underlined spaces in their place.

¿Y qué hiciste del amor que me juraste? (cloze ouline)

1. ¿Y qué _____ del amor que me _____?

2. ¿Y qué _____ de los besos que te ___?

3. ¿Y qué excusa _____ darme si _____

4. y _____ la esperanza que _____ en mí?

5. ¡Y qué ingrato ___ el destino que me _____!

6. ¡Y qué absurda la razón de mi pasión!

7. ¡Y qué necio_____ este amor que no _____

8. y _____ perdonarte tu traición!

9. Y pensar que en mi vida _____ flama

10. y el caudal de mi gloria _____ tu

11. y _____ a quererte con el alma

12. y hoy me _____ de tristeza tu actitud.

13. ¿Y a qué ____ _____, entonces, tu abandono?

14. ¿Y en qué ruta tu promesa _____?

15. Y si _____ la verdad yo te _____

16. y te _____ en mi recuerdo junto a Dios.

Repeat lines 9-16.

Preparing the Cloze Method Lesson

Set up your classroom with a CD player (or equivalent), an overhead projector (or equivalent), and a screen (or whiteboard) and follow these steps:

1 *Give out a cloze outline to each student.* Tell the students about the song: Who wrote it? Where did he/she live? When was it written? Explain to your students the point of the lesson e.g. to find verbs which are in the past and the present. The task is to listen carefully to the music as they fill in the blanks of the cloze outline.

2 *Play the song.* When you have played the song use your acetate (or whiteboard, etc.) to print in the blanks the correct answers as you elicit them from your students. If they can't find all the verbs, play the song again and ask them to have another go at it.

   (An optional or further activity might be to have them conjugate each verb [or some of the verbs] as you come to it and/or show them via acetate or paper handouts what these verbs look like when conjugated: first person singular, second person singular, etc.

3 Discuss the merits of the song.

4 **The integral text method requires more class time than the cloze method but it enables you to review many** aspects of the language. The cloze method is better suited to teaching a specific point. Since it takes less time you probably can teach two clozes in the time it would take you to do one song with the integral text method.

Projects and Reports to Present In Class

If you are teaching a whole course on love songs in Spanish (and even if you are not) you might want to assign song-related projects to your students. Here are some suggestions.

* Write an essay on the life and work of a composer, a lyricist or a recording artist. Comment on the family background. Look for things that are interesting, significant, or colorful. Simon of Simon and Garfunkel once said in an interview that one of the biggest thrills in his life was to be in Woolworth's and to hear a complete stranger humming *Bridge over Troubled Water.*

* Study the songs of a composer, lyricist or recording artist and write a report on them e.g. does he/she develop over the years? Are there certain themes which dominate? Comment on them.

* Write a book report on a book dealing with songs, a composer, a lyricist, a genre, a current in music, etc. My bibliography might suggest some possibilities.

- Search several interpretations of the same song on Youtube and evaluate them in a report.

- Find out about the origins of one of the genres: rumba/bolero, cha-cha-cha, Viennese waltz, etc. and write a report on it.

- Find a song that you like and present it to the class. Mention something about the author and his themes. Point out the merits of the song. Explain any difficult expressions. Tell them why you find this song meaningful. Print up enough copies of the song for everyone in the class.

- Find out the astrological sign of the composer, lyricist or recording artist and write an essay exploring any connections between their sign and their life and work.

- Write an essay on how a song (or songs) is/are used in the soundtrack of a movie.

Notes

Appendix

Charles Aznavour

1. Charles Aznavour's "Hier Encore" (From p. 82)

Here is a taste of Aznavour, first in the English version (surprisingly successful) then in the French original. Listen to them on YouTube–you are in for a treat.

"Hier Encore"
(*Yesterday When I Was Young*)

Yesterday when I was young

So many happy songs were waiting to be sung,

So many wild pleasures lay in store for me.

And so much pain my dazzled eyes refused to see.

I ran so fast that time and youth at last ran out.

I never stopped to think what life was all about

And every conversation I can now recall

Concerned itself with me and nothing else at all

In the original French:

Hier encore j'avais vingt ans

Je caressais le temps et jouais de la vie

Comme on joue de l'amour et je vivais la nuit

Sans compter sur mes jours qui fuyaient dans le temps.

Hier encore j'avais vingt ans.

Je gaspillais le temps en croyant l'arrêter

Et pour le retenir, et même le devancer,

Je n'ai fait que courir, et me suis essouflé.

2. "*Addio a Napoli*" by Theodoro Cottrau, Composer

Here are the words with an English translation. Google "Youtube and Addio a Napoli sung by Caruso." Lines **17** to **20** have a personal meaning for the speaker. One of the main destinations will be Argentina.

Piazza dei Martiri,
Naples, ca. 1895

25. Addio a Napoli

1. **Addio, mia bella Napoli!**
   Farewell, my beautiful Naples!

2. **Addio! Addio!**
   Farewell, Farewell!

3. **La tua suave imagine,**
   Your beautiful looks

4. **chi mai, chi mai scordar potrà?**
   Who could ever forget them?

5. **Del ciel l'azzuro fulgido,**
   The dazzling blue of the sky

6. **la placida marina,**
   The calm marina,

7. **Qual core non innebria**
   What heart do they not innebriate

8. **non bea, non bea di voluttà?**
   And bask, bask in sensual pleasure?

9. **Il ciel, la terra e l'aura**
   The sky, the land and the breeze

10. **favellano d'amore.**
    Tell of love.

11. **E solo nel mio dolore**
    And alone in my grief

Robert Stuart Thomson

12. *del porto io sognerò. Io ti sognerò.*
    Of the port I will dream. I will dream of you.
    And alone in my grief I will dream of the
    port. I will dream of you.

13. *Addio, mia bella Napoli!*
    Farewell, my beautiful Naples!

14. *Addio, addio.*
    Farewell! Farewell!

15. *Addio, care memorie*
    Farewell, dear memories

16. *del tempo che passò.*
    Of the time which has passed.

17. *Tutt'altro ciel mi chiama*
    A completely different sky calls for me

18. *Addio! addio!*
    Farewell! Farewell!

19. *Ma questo cor ti brama.*
    But this heart longs for you

20. *Il cor, il cor ti lascerò!*
    This heart, this heart I will leave with you!

21. *Di baci e d'armonia*
    Of kisses and harmony

22. *è la tua riviera.*
    Is your coast.

23. *O magica sirena,*
    Oh magic siren,

24. *fedel, fedel a te sarò!*
    Faithful, faithful to you I will be!

25 *Al mio pensier più tenero*
    To my most tender thought

26 *ritornano gli istanti,*
    Return moments,

27 *le gioie e le memorie*
    Joys and memories

28 *dei miei felici dì. I miei felici dì.*
    Of my happy days, my happy days.

(Repeat) lines 13-16 twice.

If you enjoyed listening to *Addio a Napoli* you will find more of the same in my book, "Operatic Italian". See the section "Other Books", below.

Notes

A Short Bibliography

I have mentioned key movies throughout this book. Below are some good books to enjoy.

MEXICAN CONNECTIONS

Coral, Juan Alvarez. *Compositores mexicanos (Biografías de 40 músicos desparecidos)*. Mexico City: Edamex, 1993.

Haghenbeck, F.H.. *Solamente una vez*. No information available.

Rueda, Javier Ruiz. *Agustín Lara: vida y pasiones*. Mexico City: Novara, 1976. Excellent biography with a broad historical perspective.

Wood, Andrew Grant. *Agustín Lara: a cultural biography*. Ney York City: Oxford University Press (Currents in Latin-American and Iberian Music), 2014.

INFLUENCE OF LATIN-AMERICA ON AMERICA AND VICE VERSA

Morales, Ed. *The Latin Beat*. Cambridge: Da Capo Press, 2009. Traces the influence of Latin rhythms on music in the United States.

Patten, James. *Latin Sounds of the Past: Original Recordings (1927-1941)*. Los Angeles: *Take Two Records*, 2001. This CD package comes with a cogent fifteen page outline of the golden age (approx. 1930-1955) of Latin-American music.

Roberts, John Storm. *The Impact of Latin American Music on the United States*. New York: Oxford, 1999.

RECORDING ARTISTS

Gourse, Leslie. *The Life and Mystique of Nat King Cole*. New York: St. Martin's Press, 1991. A fine detailed biography.

Snowman, Daniel. *Plácido Domingo's Tales from the Opera*. Portland, OR: Amadeus Press, 1995.

TANGO

Benatar, Asher. *Tango*. Buenos Aires: Ars, 1992. The text is in Spanish and English. The photographs are works of art.

Denniston, Christine. *The Meaning of Tango: The Story of the Argentinian Dance.* London: Portico Books, 2007.

Rial, Horacio. *Las dos muertes de Gardel.* Buenos Aires: Vázquez, 2001.

GENERAL

Diccionario didáctico avanzado. Mexico City: SM de Ediciones, 2010. An excellent guide for the reader who is interested in subtle definitions, etymologies, etc. and who enjoys jumping in at the deep end and thinking in Spanish.

OTHER

El español y los siete pecados capitales Madrid: Alianza, 1966, Ch.1.

Neumeyer, D. and others. "Music and Cinema". Middletown: Wesleyan University Press, 2000.

Acknowledgments

The author wishes to thank Mr. Asher Benatar for his generous permission to use a few photographs from his book, *Tango*.

Robert Stuart Thomson

Other Books by Robert Stuart Thomson

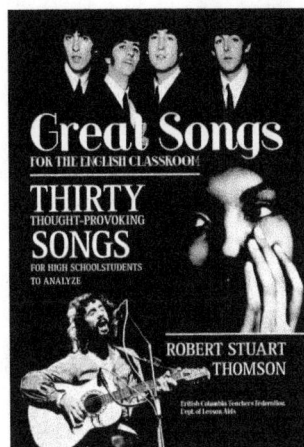

Great Songs for the English Classroom (1980). Thirty thought-provoking songs for high school students to analyze. Students listen to the songs and print the missing words on cloze outlines. This is followed by a class discussion and journal writing. Working on songs develops listening skills, provides a review of basics (spelling, vocabulary) and offers the student a forum in which to explore important issues such as love, friendship, peer pressure, parental neglect, alienation, and anger. This book was published by the British Columbia Teachers Federation Dept. of Lesson Aids.

Italian for the Opera (1991). 150 pages, with black and white photos. Examines in depth many extracts from operas and discusses subtleties such as connotation, layers of meaning, and aspects of the composer which surface in the text. At the same time, it analyses in logical order parts of speech. Includes quizzes to monitor progress plus an index. This book sold out in 2003 after an initial print run of 2000 and has recently (2013) been reprinted.

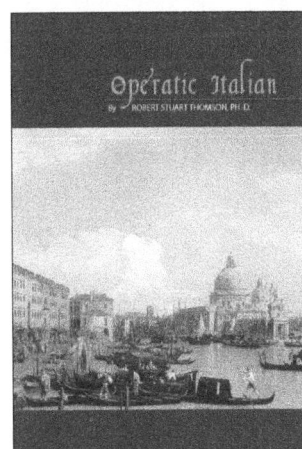

Operatic Italian (2009). 460 pages, with many photos and IPA used throughout. A huge expansion of "Italian for the Opera", this book contains several new chapters: how to study operatic Italian on your own, the sounds and rhythm of Italian, suitable esthetic criteria for judging operatic Italian, what to read for good plot outlines, the pros and cons of subtitles, the influence of Dante, operatic language in canzoni, a brief look at Neapolitan.

"*Operatic Italian* would make a fantastic textbook for a conservatory or university." — Sarah Luebke, *Opera Today*, 2010.

All of these books can be seen and ordered on my website:
www.godwinbooks.com.

You will find on my site the table of contents, sample passages from the books, and reviews by critics. Order these books — paperback or eBook — online or mail your cheque to Robert Thomson: PO Box 50021, Victoria, B.C. Canada V8S 5L8.

Photos on the Cover

The numbers in parentheses refer to the songs

Top, left to right:
Plácido Domingo, Osvaldo Farrés (4), Nana Mouskouri (18), Lola Beltrán (8, 16), Vicente Fernández (6, 12), Alvaro Carrillo Alarcón (10).

Second row, left to right:
Ernesto Lecuona (7), Javier Solís (14), Cervantes, Gabriel Ruiz (2), Mario de Jesús Báez (14), Luis Miguel (14)

Bottom row, left to right:
Eydie Gorme (2, 3, 10), Agustín Lara (1, 3, 17), Al Pacino (22), Carlos Gardel (11, 20, 21), Manuelita Arriola (1), Julio Iglesias (19, 22)

Robert Stuart Thomson

www.ingramcontent.com/pod-product-compliance
Lightning Source LLC
Chambersburg PA
CBHW081152090426
42736CB00017B/3288